S0-AZI-812

BURAKUMIN:
A JAPANESE MINORITY AND EDUCATION

BURAKUMIN:
A JAPANESE MINORITY
AND EDUCATION

by

NOBUO SHIMAHARA

MARTINUS NIJHOFF / THE HAGUE / 1971

PRINTED IN THE NETHERLANDS

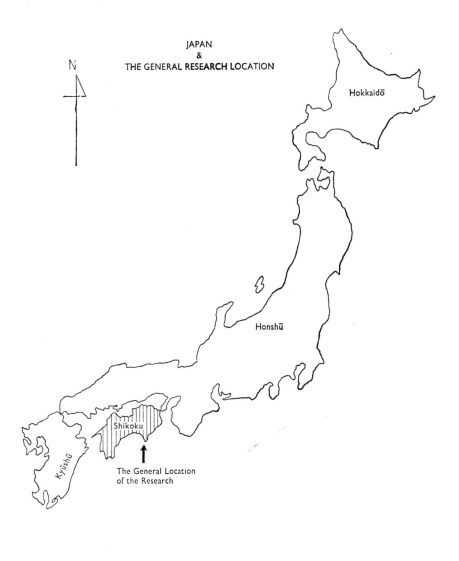

JAPAN
&
THE GENERAL RESEARCH LOCATION

N

Hokkaidō

Honshū

Shikoku

Kyūshū

The General Location
of the Research

TABLE OF CONTENTS

ACKNOWLEDGMENTS

It was Professor George Spindler at Stanford University who encouraged me to write this case study. I wish to express my gratitude to him for his insightful suggestions and criticisms which were indeed valuable to the undertaking of my work. I am particularly grateful to Professor Theodore Brameld at the University of Hawaii for his continuous encouragement and generous assistance without which my field work could not have been completed.

I would also like to express my appreciation to the following persons for their assistance during my field work and writing: Professor Hiroyoshi Inai, Professor Shigeharu Matsuura, Professor David Conrad, Professor Adam Scrupski, and Miss Midori Matsuyama. My gratitude cannot be fully expressed in words to my informants whose cooperation made possible my project in Japan as well as this case study. Unfortunately I am not able to name them here since their names must be kept confidential.

I am deeply indebted to the Wenner-Gren Foundation for Anthropological Research who assisted to finance my Japanese research for one year from 1964 to 1965. Finally I appreciate the generosity of the Random House who allowed me to make a quotation from: Edwin Reischauer, *Beyond Vietnam: the United States and Asia.*

New Brunswick, New Jersey   N.S.
October, 1970

INTRODUCTION

This is a profile of people known as Burakumin, a Japanese minority group with a history of many centuries. The Burakumin is an "invisible race" which, unlike the Negro and other races in America, lacks stigma of color or other physical distinctions. Not invisible is it otherwise, for Burakumin are unlike the majority Japanese in a variety of cultural features historically derivative from discrimination and prejudice which Burakumin have long suffered.

This study of Burakumin focused on the responses of two compulsory schools to the problems of this minority group. Other research foci were integrated into this central concern of the study so as to provide a unified cultural perspective. Attention was given to such various aspects of Burakumin culture as: historical perspective, community life, struggles for emancipation, organizational activities, nature of prejudice and discrimination, attitudes and responses of non-Burakumin towards Burakumin.

Education in its broadest sense is an indigenous cultural process by means of which the culture, whether literate or non-literate, can maintain its continuity; this process is widely woven into the complex fabric of man's life and his organized activities. Education in a formal sense, however, is institutionalized schooling engaged in cultural transmission and change. One of the practical advantages of studying education in an anthropological perspective is to treat it in the matrix of culture as education and culture relate to each other. The present study focused its attention upon formal education with only minor attention given to informal aspects.

Research was conducted for approximately one year from 1964 to 1965 in Eizen city, Kagada prefecture, Shikoku, Japan. The community selected for our study was Junan, a dynamic ghetto of Burakumin infused with high sensitivity toward their problems and involved in a wide range of intra- and inter-group conflicts. The dynamics of this community were our special interest particularly in view of the fact that Japanese culture has been undergoing dynamic change. Yonami Elementary School and Tōzai Junior High School were chosen for the research primarily because they accommodate Junan students.

The present case study was a part of the author's Japanese research which also involved a fishing village in a neighboring city and two other schools connected with the village. This case study, however, excludes treatment of the fishing village. The author's research was part of a larger Japanese study directed by Professor Theodore Brameld (Brameld 1968: 267–277) in which the author participated as a member of the Brameld research team. From this participation the present case study was greatly benefited.

Fictitious names were given to all persons, institutions, the Burakumin community, the city, and the prefecture involved in this study in order to conceal the actual location of the research and the real names of respondents.

We established our residence near the heart of Eizen geographically close enough to maintain maximum communication with Junan Burakumin, the two schools, the municipal school board, the city hall, and the respondents in Eizen. Although our panel of respondents was limited to students, teachers, and administrators in the two schools and on the school board, as well as close educational associations in Eizen, the source of the data used in this case study includes not only this panel but also a larger panel of our research team representing five institutions: the recreational, political, economic, religious, and educational.

The major research method used was intensive interviews. In addition to formal interviews, the following were also employed as frequently as possible in order to obtain relevant data and access to the life of Burakumin and the process of the schools: participant observation, group discussion, informal supplementary interviews, informal visits to homes, meetings, festivities, and schools, and the study of documents and literature.

Beginning with a brief preview of Japanese culture and education, this case study will continue in Chapters Two and Three with a history of the Burakumin and the Junan community. Education and its responses to Burakumin problems will be considered in Chapters Four and Five. Finally Chapter Six will provide a short conclusion.

As a final word of introduction, it should be noted that the author is Japanese and has lived in Japan for 24 years. He admits forth-rightly that he may not always have been objective in presenting the data because of his cultural background. At the same time he hopes his background enriched this case study.

CHAPTER ONE

JAPAN IN TRANSITION: CULTURE AND EDUCATION

Two and a half centuries of Tokugawa feudalism (1603–1867) contributed to the long isolation of Japan from the stream of cultural diffusion. Feudal leaders enjoyed political peace and tranquility during this dormancy of Japanese history. But tranquility did not last forever since Japan confronted the powerful impact of Western cultures in the last half of the nineteenth century. Since then change became a vital force of Japanese society. This chapter is an introductory Survey of Japanese culture and education in transition.

Since Meiji

Japan has celebrated the centennial of her era of modernization which began in 1868. The past century has been a dramatic period of Japanese history, characterized by a staggering speed of transition. It has been a "dialectical" process of social development with pendulum–like swings from one position to another – of recurrent shifts from theses of cultural oscillation to antitheses to syntheses.

This dramatic century was divided into three formal chronologies since the inception of the Meiji period in 1868 which ended Tokugawa feudalism. The Meiji period, the first revolutionary era which shattered feudalism and its social structure, was the reign of Emperor Mutsuhito (1868–1912). The Taishō period (1912–1926) was less colorful and dramatic; it was the period of Emperor Yoshihito. The Shōwa era, designated as the period of Emperor Hirohito (1926–   ), has two features: the prewar and postwar periods. Both drastically determined the course of Japan in two diametrically opposed directions. The first path was national polity and the second, democracy and peace.

The changes of political ideology may well reveal the dialectical processes of these eras. Beginning with the Meiji Restoration, the relaxation of feudalism was soon accompanied by overwhelming Westernization and Meiji enlightenment while, in the later Meiji, ideological restraints were created by the rise of nationalism and Confucian traditionalism. The Taishō era called for political freedom, although for a short span of time, creating an ideological relaxation during which the Japanese Socialist party was developed. It was also in this period that Marxism was introduced to Japan for the first time. Shortly after the Taishō, the Shōwa restraints precipitated by the Manchurian incident in 1931, were introduced with the subsequent result of ultramilitaristic dominance in later years. The year 1945 was a time of more profound social dislocation and deeper personal shock than the Meiji Restoration since it was an historical moment of defeat and destruction deeply pervading all spheres of Japanese life. The Japanese had never before experienced such disintegration. At the same time, this defeat contributed to another relaxation of ideological mood. At present, two decades later since then, nationalism is a growing concern of many Japanese in the postwar period of the Shōwa.

Contemporary Change

Describing the development of Japan, Edwin Reischauer (1967: 109–110), an American expert of Japanese history, says:

> Modern Japan teaches a more hopeful lesson about the survival of non-Western cultures. In the early days of Japan's modernization, it seemed that the native culture was being swept away by a tidal wave of Westernization. Japan, some people felt, would become a rootless Asian outpost of Western civilization. As we look at the situation today, however, we see how strong Japanese cultural traits remain. Japan is without doubt the most culturally distinctive of the modernized nations. It is exceedingly Japanese.

Japan is indeed exceedingly Japanese. At the same time Japanese culture is characterized by a contrast between its tradition and new acculturated traits.

Some sketchy illustrations may be relevant here. In large Japanese cities, there are countless English-written neon signs and front windows of small stores as well as mammoth department stores and business offices standing side by side. Labels of medicine and cosmetics are printed in large English letters with small Japanese letters under English labels as subtitles. Even fertilizer containers and rural barber shops have salient English signs, occasionally spelled wrong. Restaurants and Western style hotels not only in such sophisticated, complex cities as Tokyo, Kyoto, and Osaka, but also in relatively remote local cities of one-tenth of a million population are frequently identified by conspicuous English signs at the entrance.

Japanese industry has succeeded in achieving a mass production of automobiles elevating itself to the second place in 1968 in the world automobile production. Among numerous passenger automobiles there is not a single car with Japanese or Chinese symbols designating the name of the car. These symbols are either English or romanized. Additionally most automobile parts are designated in English.

In music, American jazz and popular songs are prevalent all over Japan. They are often sung by Japanese singers in the native American language. In art, Western models of painting are widely adopted and practiced by students at the college level as well as by professionals. This is obvious in art exhibitions in universities, art galleries, and museums with growing orientations toward Western art. Some Japanese artists believe that the creation of a unique synthesis incorporating both Western arts and the contributions of indigenous Japanese aesthetics is essential.

The dominant pattern of clothing worn by urban dwellers is not dissimilar to that of American urban dwellers. Private houses combining both Western and Japanese styles are increasingly built for urban dwellers, particularly for those who are called Sarariiman (salaried men who are white collar workers).

The Japanese educational system is almost the same as the American system with its inception in 1947. Although some notable changes were introduced since the educational reformation of 1947, the main structural features of the system at least have been still maintained. Those who criticize the system as an American imposition under the American Occupation Administration have been more vocal recently claiming that the system must be changed to fit the needs of the Japanese socio-cultural systems. It is not, however, likely that a drastic structural change will occur soon.

Japanese acculturation prevails far more widely and ruthlessly in various realms of Japanese culture such as art, music, business, technology, recreation, literature, movie industry, and education.

Despite this fact, Japanese culture, as Reischauer says, retains its original forms in a number of ways as expressed, for example, in aesthetics and patterns of thought – basic Japanese aesthetic concepts such as the feeling for color, space, and asymmetry; woodblock prints, pottery, gardening, interior decorating, poetry, drama, architecture, and flower arrangement; Zen and sports influenced by Zen philosophy such as Jūdō, Kendō (Japanese fencing), and Karate.

Yet what makes Japanese remarkably different from other Oriental cultures, in the eyes of Western people at least, may not be Japanese culture's retainability of its tradition but perhaps its amenability to change and its resilience.

The superstructures of the political, judicial, and religious, and the systems of Japanese economy and industry were abolished when Japan was surrendered to the Allied Powers in 1945. Among many institutions of Japanese culture, economy has recovered most remarkably. Its annual median growth rate in the past one and a half decade is over 12 per cent, its maximum rate being over 17 per cent in 1959. Japan's G.N.P. topped Britain's in 1967 and is approaching West Germany's G.N.P. Japan has become the third industrial nation behind the United States and the Soviet Union.

Japan enjoys the highest rate of literacy in the world. Seventy-five per cent of the junior high school (compulsory) graduates enter senior high schools, with very few subsequent dropouts. In Tokyo 90 per cent of junior high school graduates enter senior high schools. One out of every four senior high school graduates goes to college through high competition imposed by the college entrance examination system. In 1967 the Japanese colleges and universities including both public and private institutions admitted 60 per cent of 730,000 total applicants although the regular accomodation capacity of the entire higher institutions was only 290,000 students a year.

Japan has seen a vital religious movement since the end of the last war. The Sōkagakkai, one of the Nichiren Buddhist sects, originated before the Second World War and revitalized during the early postwar period of social dislocation and valuational crisis, is a powerful, politically oriented organization which is reported to enroll 15 million devoted members. The astonishing phenomenon of this movement is the growth of the organization from a minute group soon after the war to the most militant and largest religious organization. It is attractive particularly to the lower-middle and lower socio-economic segment of the Japanese population. As of 1967 the Sōkagakkai succeeded in seating 25 members in the Lower House of Representatives and 20 members in the Upper House of Councilors. It is reported that it won a far greater number of seats in the Japanese Diet in the latest elections held in 1969.

Japan has achieved a high degree of political stability despite the unusual postwar social turmoil. There has been a drastic change in Japanese politics from the prewar totalitarianism to a democratic system which started in the vortex of political and social dislocation caused both internally and externally by conflicting orientations.

At present comprised of four major islands, Honshū, Kyūshū, Shikoku, and Hokkaidō, with numerous tiny islands scattering around these main islands, Japan embraces 42 prefectures in addition to Osaka, Kyoto, Tokyo, and Hokkaidō. Although each prefecture is administratively equivalent to a state in America, geographically it is more or less similar to a county. It has political autonomy to a degree but in its function it is a part of the larger political umbrella of the national government. The latter with its ministerial cabinet at the top appointed by the prime minister who is usually the chief of the ruling party has great power over the prefectural governments; with a similar hierarchical structure of political power the prefectural government controls counties and cities to a great extent. A certain degree of political autonomy is, nevertheless, given to local cities, towns, villages headed by municipal and town mayors or village chiefs.

Demographically there has been a consistent trend of population increase in urban areas. In 1965, more than 68 per cent of the 98 million Japanese population dwelt in urban areas according to the national census. Agricultural population has been declining with a steady rate in recent years. The agricultural population of 1967 including full- and part-time farmers and their dependents dropped to 28,640,000, a decrease of three per cent from 1965. It constituted less than 30 per cent of the total population for the first time. On the other hand, the fishing population including unemployed dependents comprised no more than two per cent. It has been diminishing as the petit scale of fishing has been in the gradual process of decrease. One phenomenal change in fishing in 1966 may attest to the above evidence: fishing involving sailing boats and coastal trawlers declined by 17 per cent since the previous year. The present policy of the national government is to minimize both the agricultural and fishing population without the decline of production by introducing efficient mechanical devices. Meanwhile it intends to increase employed population in secondary and tertiary industries (industries related to processing and manufacturing such as marine processing, textile manufacture, heavy industry; economic activities other than those categorized in primary and secondary industries such as commerce, finance, "service business," transportation).

According to the national census of 1965, the distribution of 47,610,000 Japanese engaged in full-time productive activities in three types of industry was: 24.6 per cent involved in primary industry (economic activities for obtaining raw materials such as agriculture, fishing, forestry); 32.3 per cent in secondary industry; 43 per cent in tertiary industry.

Turning briefly to the family, the average number of members has become smaller by Japan's effort to control the family size. This is evidenced, for example, by the contrast of the average family number, 4.45 persons in 1960 with 4.05 in 1965.

The traditionally dominant family pattern is unilateral patrilineage composed of the descendants of a male ancestor. It still prevails in Japanese society, but more dominantly in the agricultural and fishing communities than in the urban, industrial areas.

The family pattern of the Ube fishing community (Shimahara 1967: 29–73) may serve as an example of the surviving traditional pattern. The first son of a fisherman inherits his father's ancestral property accompanied by a subsequent obligation to provide security for living for his parents and grandparents under the same shelter. If there is no son, the first daughter may become the inheritor. The first son's wife, parents, grandparents, and siblings live together as a corporate unit of family. His siblings ready for independence are given three paths: (1) marriage with inheritors of other families; (2) establishment of independent families in the same community; (3) establishment of independent families in urban areas.

The inherited house is called Honke symbolizing the perpetuity of ancestral life for a number of generations. Meanwhile, adult sons other than the first, when ready to establish separate families in Ube, are offered economic assistance by Honke to varying degrees contingent upon its economic ability. These separate families are called branch houses, or Bunke. The ordinary relationship between Honke and Bunke is that of loyalty of the latter to the former, and in turn, a generous paternalism of Honke is expected by Bunke. Mutuality between them for economic activities and in case of emergency is paramount. In Ube, Bunke and Honke sons occasionally organize fishing teams at the request of the latter. However, Bunke maintains independent economic units. Similar relationships between Honke and Bunke also prevails in agricultural communities.

One new growing trend is the increase of nuclear families. In 1965, of the total 24,080,000 households in the nation, nuclear families consisting of parents and their children were 10,490,000 and the families of only couples were 2,260,000. As compared with 1960, the former increased by 23.6 per cent while the latter, by 38.8 per cent.

Changes in value-orientations have been occurring, not only in families, but also in wider institutions such as education, economy, politics, religion, and labor. Under the Occupation Administration of the late 1940's, not only structural transformations but also subsequent changes in patterns of values have been virtually immersed. Thus although feudalism and authoritarianism remained deeply woven into the fabric of Japanese social structure, indoctrination of concepts of democracy and individual freedom was also promoted. Postwar schools have taught such concepts with little attention to traditional ethical concepts like filial piety, ancestral worship, Giri (traditional notion of mutual obligation), and On (obligation to people with seniority statuses such as parents and senior members of a group). Women were emancipated to a significant degree from the shackles of male-dominated authoritarianism and children have been given an appreciable recognition in the family. Feudal tenants were freed while labor became active and militant. There has been a notable transition of human relations orientations from "lineality" to "collaterality" emphasizing what David Reisman called other-directed orientations. As a result of discontinuity in value-orientations, conflicts tend to occur between the older and younger generations.

Finally, a brief reference to Burakumin previously referred to as a minority group. In the phenomenal change of Japanese culture and in the progress of Japanese economy, this minority group and their life have been largely ignored by the majority of the Japanese. They are a group that has been least benefited in the development of Japanese society. Their existence is hardly recognized by societies outside Japan. Yet they have inherited a distinct history, and unforgettable past; they are still living in this history and in a discriminated culture.

As Japan was approaching the end of the Taisho period (the early 1920's), the Japanese Socialist movement and Marxism helped to create a drastic turning point in the struggles of Burakumin for emancipation. Under the influence of socialist orientations, Burakumin organized the first self-directed national organization and began to systematically and collectively attack numerous incidents of discrimination and governmental policies. Their protests against discrimination until that time had been rather spontaneous and sporadic. Although leading non-Burakumin social reformers in the Meiji era advocated Burakumin liberation, little tangible effect was achieved. Despite the fact that the national Burakumin organization has considerably contributed since its inception to the sensitization of both Burakumin and non-Burakumin toward the social reality of prejudice and discrimination in a variety of ways, the heart of prejudice against Burakumin has been dissolved little.

Prewar Education

We have sketched the transformation of Japanese culture. Let us now pay brief attention to Japanese education in transition.

Formal education has undergone a rapid change since the Meiji Restoration no less than other aspects of Japanese culture. Postwar education features a radical departure from prewar education. There are two distinct developmental phases in the former while five in the latter. The latter will be considered first.

The first nation-wide, modern educational system in Japanese history was instituted in 1872. This was four years after the revolutionary Meiji Restoration had begun to uproot the social structure of Tokugawa feudalism. The establishment of the universal educational system characterized the first stage in the prewar education, most significant in the evolution of Japanese formal education. It aroused heated controversies among progressive and conservative intellectuals. There were three influential groups whose arguments rested upon three different ideological sources (Morito 1961: 3). The first, the Kyoto group, insisted that the primary emphasis of education should be put on the Japanese classics. Opposing the Kyoto view was the Tokyo group contending that education should be based on the Chinese classics and Confucianism, the core of Tokugawa education during the feudal period. As is well known, Confucianism was a major source of ethics in Japanese culture. Against the continuity of Tokugawa education in the Meiji era, the most influential progressive group argued in favor of Western education. They maintained that a Western educational system should be introduced into Japanese education at the founding of the new Japan. Their view was the most innovative and appealing to those leaders eager to incorporate Western ideas into Japanese culture. It was this progressive Western group that succeeded in taking leadership in the attempt to institutionalize the new educational system.

French and American education was the major source of influence.

While the structure of the new educational system was organized from the model of the French educational system, the contents were taken from American education. Elementary school education was the central concern of education in the new system. Its curriculum was the direct translation of the American curriculum at the elementary school level.

The second stage is distinguished by a swing toward traditionalism. Between 1872 and 1886, there had been a growing traditionalism and a rise of nationalism in education. These were seen in the form of militant reactions to Western-oriented education. The reaction represented by traditionalism was the criticism by conservative intellectuals of the development of "individualism" which was encouraged by the new education.

A further modification took place in 1880 incorporating the ideology of the Japanese classic school represented by Eifu Motoda, the most eloquent spokesman of the Emperor, by replacing liberal elements with Confucianism. At this time Shūsin (moral education) was introduced.

The fusion of Confucianism and nationalism featured the third stage. The development of nationalism was precipitated through Japan's confrontation with advanced Western nations. It was the contention of the nationalists that more attention should be given to the integrity and survival of the state than to the development of individuals and their freedom advocated by the Western-oriented group. In 1890, Tsuyoshi Inoue, an ardent advocate of nationalism wrote the draft of the Imperial Rescript on Education in collaboration with Eifu Motoda, the most influential exponent of Confucianist ethics. In October, this was promulgated as the "spiritual framework of education for the Tennō (Emperor) system."

Despite the upsurge of nationalism, a fourth stage occurred in the Taishō period which produced a partial swing back to the early Meiji reconstruction by providing further opportunities for the expansion of freedom and the diffusion of Western ideologies. But it was not merely a return to the earlier liberal stage, for another innovation occurred: the diffusion of Marxism into Japanese culture and its application to Japanese pedagogy. The studies of Marxism and its influence upon pedagogical thought reached a peak in the second half of the 1920's.

Finally, the fifth stage brought a period of totalitarian control to education. Liberal and radical thought advocated by intellectuals in the Taishō period was destined to be suppressed in the 1930's. The period between the Manchurian Incident (1931) and the Chinese-Japanese War (1937) was a critical time when the national government attempted to exterminate radical thought and at the same time to build pedagogical theories of Kokutai Shugi (nationalism for the development of the Emperor state). These theories were systematized further and practiced in the next period from the Chinese-Japanese War to the end of World War II.

Postwar Showa Reform

The Second World War finally ended when Japan accepted the Potsdam Declaration on August 15, 1945. The foundations of prewar Showa education for the Emperor state were uprooted. In the last half of the 1940's, therefore, Japanese education was radically changed under the supervision of the Allied Powers by the enactment of five new educational laws – the Fundamental Law of Education (1947), the School Education Law (1947), the School Board Law (1948), the Law Concerning Public Teachers (1949), and the Social Education Law (1949).

The most comprehensive reform of Japanese education was designed in 1946 by the United States Education Mission headed by George Stoddard. An historically meaningful fact of the reform was that the Education Mission provided a prototype of democratic education which had never been formulated previously in the development of Japanese culture. It was a radical innovation transplanted into Japanese education.

Among the recommendations for the educational reform by the Mission the following were most significant: first it emphasized administrative decentralization. Second, it proposed a new single-track school system consisting of elementary education for six years, lower secondary education for three years, upper secondary education for three years, and higher education. This proposal became a model for the creation of the 6-3-3-4 system which came into full operation in 1949 under the School Law. Compulsory education under this law was extended to nine years from six years in the prewar Showa education system. Additionally, the conception of democracy was introduced into the curriculum. The Mission also stressed: the creation of greater opportunities for liberal education at higher levels; adult education; language reform; democratic methods of teaching.

In order to renovate Japanese education according to this framework, the Education Reform Committee was organized in 1946. This Japanese agency has played one of the most innovative roles in changing Japanese education. The theoretical foundations of the educational reformation were framed in the Fundamental Law of Education which emphasized the growth of individual personality, academic freedom, equality of education, general education as a nine-year compulsory program, coeducation, social education, and democracy in school administration.

As mentioned previously, there are two phases in the postwar education. The first is the formative period of the reformation; the other, the reaction to the reformation which started early in the fifties.

Concepts and methods formulated by American progressivists such as John Dewey and William Kilpatrick exerted influence upon formative Japanese education. Emphasized in educational process were active learning such as problem solving, child's self-activity and interest, freedom, and self-expression. Club activities, home room, and guidance attracted considerable attention as new concepts of extracurricular activity. Another new concept of education was the notion of the community school.

Japanese teachers endeavored to put the new orientations into practice. In the formative period, the schools were regarded as community institutions for innovations. They were used for a variety of community purposes; teachers and students were involved in community studies; teachers participated in organizational activities of women and young men. In the curriculum, controversial issues of the communities and the nation were given a significant place for treatment. Furthermore critical, reflective attitudes of the students and the development of their sensitivity toward social problems were encouraged.

Within three or four years after the introduction of progressivist education, negative reactions, however, began to grow. Hence a crucial transformation in teaching and learning methods took place in the first half of the fifties, which was a significant shift from experimentalist orientations in methods to essentialist orientations stressing behavioristic, passive learning, logical order of knowledge rather than child's experience, acquiry in learning rather than inquiry. There was a marked transformation of roles of the schools which occurred around 1952. These changes were indicative of the inception of the phase of reaction.

In the period of reaction and stabilization, the schools have become agents for intellectual conditioning. Most of the learning took place within the four walls of a classroom; above all, a passive reinforcement of learning was emphasized through frequent tests which, in turn, were aimed, to a great extent, at the preparation for examinations for higher educational institutions. Most Japanese schools devoted themselves largely to the effective transmission of descriptive and traditional knowledge and facts. They functioned as formal intellectual agents of cultural transmission isolated from community processes.

Another important transformation in Japanese education was a change in the control of education. Two new laws were enacted in 1956 which are aimed at the concentration of power in the national government. In the formative period, the decentralization of educational control was considered as a form of democratic control, one of the most significant features of the postwar education reform. This principle of decentralization was abolished when the two laws were enacted. One was concerned with the restriction of political activities of teachers; the other was a new "school board law" which superseded the reformation school board law of 1948. Since then centralization has been a developing phenomenon.

Another significant change in the history of postwar Japanese education was the revival of moral education in 1958. Formulated to fill the "moral vacuum" of the Japanese caused, it was claimed, by the loss of moral identity, it was not a replica of the prewar moral education which source was the Emperial Rescript on Education and Shūshin, but rather democratic in its basic character. One of the motivations of reinstating moral education, however, was derived from an appeal to the traditional Japanese character and moral sources. Thus a long series of debates arose among intellectuals over moral education in both the academic domain and in the National Diet, reflecting conflicts of ideologies and emerging thought in postwar Japanese culture. After nearly ten years of controversy, the Ministry of Education decided in 1957 that moral education would be incorporated as a separate subject into the elementary and junior high school curricula.

As seen above, the trend in the period of reaction and stabilization is an antithesis to education of the formative period which has been continuing to the present time.

One more important and prefatory note is needed here regarding a new development of the postwar education. There have been efforts of voluntary associations and the Ministry of Education to cope, within the framework of education, with problems of Japanese outcastes. Dōwa (peaceful assimilation) education has been designated to such efforts. It existed unsystematically and informally before the last war. It was only in the fifties that organized attempts have been made to develop Dōwa education in the structure of formal education. Dōwa education is significant in Japanese education since it addresses itself to minority problems which had been neglected for many centuries in the history of the Japanese culture. Our particular concern here is to inquire into the extent to which our two schools are responding to Dōwa education. Further attention shall be given to its dynamics and history in later chapters.

CHAPTER TWO

THE BURAKUMIN AS A MINORITY

Discriminated Japanese

The Japanese minority called Burakumin, to which we referred in the preceding chapter, are scattered throughout 4,000 communities in 29 prefectures. The total population of the Burakumin is estimated at between 1,500,000 and 2,500,000 (De Vos, Wagatsuma, 1966: 177).

Burakumin is a shortened name for Tokushu Burakumin, literally meaning special village people. They are occasionally called Eta (meaning defilement abundant) behind the backs of Burakumin or sometimes even to their faces. They are "special people" because they had been treated legally as "outcastes" during the long Tokugawa Period of two and a half centuries (1603–1867). Although they were given a new status, Shin Heimin (new commoners), equivalent to the status of the other commoners by the Emancipation Edict of 1871, their actual life has changed only moderately in many decades.

The terms Burakumin or Buraku no Hito (persons of Buraku) are usually cited in public by both Burakumin and non-Burakumin. The term Eta, however, is a derogatory one, inducing hostility towards Burakumin when used by a non-Burakumin. Furthermore, there are many other names referring to the Burakumin, as told to us by a Burakumin manager of a block factory. They are invidiously called Yottsu (four). Its etymology is in the term Shinhei Min, referred to above. "Shi" implies four, which is pronounced "Yottsu" in Japanese. The notion of "Yottsu" is also associated with "four legs" of the animal which symbolically refer to the supposedly subhuman attributes of Burakumin. (De Vos, Wagatsuma 1966: 4). In Kyoto and Osaka, "Renga" (bricks) is used occasionally; there "four" bricks are tied together when bricks are shipped out from factories. In Nagasaki, Burakumin are also referred to by a different name – Mukōjima (an island on the opposite side). Years ago, according to the Burakumin manager, Burakumin were hated because they were eating meat of cattle and horses. As eating meat was considered to be a "dirty custom," they were exiled to an island where they became permanent residents. These terms are illustrative of the non-Burakumin's attitude toward Burakumin.

Historical Background

Systems of social stratification of small "nations" in Japan had been organized as early as the first century. Slavery was a common practice and slaves were assigned to various occupational specializations. In the eighth century after the Taika Restoration (701), people were categorized into two main divisions: Ryomin (good people) and Senmin (lowly people). There were five types of Senmin classified according to occupational specialization: Ryoto (tomb guards), Kanko (government cultivators), Kunuhi (government servants), Shinuhi (private slaves), and Genin (temple and private slaves). Additionally there was a group called Zakko who were treated as semi-Senmin even though their official status was higher than that of Senmin. They were assigned to special occupations requiring high skills, such as leather work, tanning, cloth dyeing, shoemaking, weapons manufacture, etc. It was Senmin and Zakko who advanced sophisticated Japanese arts by creating beautiful artifacts.

Among Zakko, there were Etori, who were engaged in gathering food for the hawks and dogs used by aristocrats for hunting in the Department of Falconry called the Takatsukasa. With the dissemination of Buddhism, first introduced to Japan in 538 through China and Korea, the Takatsukasa was temporarily abolished in 757 and finally disbanded in 860. Etori, accordingly, became butchers whose main work was slaughter. Their occupation was despised after an edict prohibiting the slaughter of horses and cattle was enforced in 676 under the influence of Buddhism. Historians trace the etymology of Eta to Etori (Inoue 1964: 17). The corruption of Etori is Eto. A further corruption of Eto became Eta.

When the Ritsuryo system – the social and political system originated in 645 – broke down at the end of the eighth century, the Senmin status system began to collapse. As a consequence, many Do-Hi (male and female slaves) escaped into other communities, crossing jurisdictional boundaries. One of the results of this social upheaval was intermarriage between citizens and Do-Hi. Although the slaves were not taxed under the Senmin status system, it was decided in 798 that, due to the need for additional tax income, offspring born as a result of intermarriages were to be considered as taxable citizens. This was the first emancipation of Senmin. At the beginning of the tenth century, the Do-Hi institutional system was repealed. The abolition of the system was merely nominal, similar to the Emancipation Edict of 1871 which was nothing less than tokenism since it did not change appreciably the legal and economic structure of the society. Senmin remained in the same occupations under the control of manorial lords.

During the Chūse Period (1192–1603), there had been great social upheaval. As political and manorial powers of feudal lords were weakening in the twelfth century, Bushi (warriors) arose as new powers, thus gaining political influence all over Japan. Furthermore, rivalry of influential Bushi had continued as a result of power struggles, with consequent alterations in governments controlled by Bushi. During this period, the constituency of Senmin was significantly altered. Successful Senmin and serfs became landlords or full-fledged farmers, whereas declining landlords, serfs, and Bushi fell into the category of Senmin. Owing to the social upheaval of the Chūse Period which caused the intermingling of Senmin with others, Senmin of this period were not identical with those whose status had been stabilized in the previous centuries (Inoue 1964: 18).

The jobs which were considered to be "lowly" and "dirty" were assigned to Seminin. Among these were various manufactures including pottery, tanning, leatherwork, and mat and bamboo craft, entertainment, itinerant singing, peddling, marine transportation, gardening, ditch and well digging, public execution, cattle breeding. Senmin residential areas were often found on the banks of rivers or on barren land within the precincts of manors. Such areas were called Sanjo, a name some Burakumin ghettoes still retain. Many Sanjo were concentrated at key transportation points where Senmin laborers engaging in transportation rested. Besides these laborers, beggars, disposers of the dead, public executors, and other Senmin gathered in Sanjo. Those who were engaged in "lowly and dirty" occupations described above were called by different names during the Chūse Period such as Sanjo whose term was originally used to refer to their residence, Kawara Mono, and Yado no Mono. Until the fourteenth century, Sanjo was the most popular term used to designate the Japanese pariah group that included both Eta and Hinin (public executors, disposers of the dead).

The Formation of Burakumin

These Senmin thus contributed to the historical development of Burakumin. There was a certain degree of mobility in the Japanese pariah group, and some Sanjo passed into other communities. However, in the sixteenth century, they were fixed to specific residential areas where mobility was forbidden. Imakawa, a Samurai ruler, for example, gathered skilled lowly people on a bank to form a community of leather workers. In other cases, Kawara Mono were forced to concentrate near a castle to form a community of skilled workers needed by a Samurai ruler. Hence they were simultaneously subjected to a rigid fixation of occupational specializations, residential areas, and a particular status. The fixation of these three factors, although not as rigid as in the Tokugawa Period, contributed to the formation of what is now called Tokushu Buraku or special Burakumin community. It served as a prototype of the Tokugawa status system. Thus, under farmers in the sixteenth century there were Eta, Hinin, mixed Senmin, and similar pariah groups called Yado no Mono, Hachiya, Chasen, Onbo, and Tonai.

The final shaping of Burakumin status occurred with the development of the Tokugawa status system. This consisted of four hierarchical strata: aristocrats and warriors, farmers, artisans, and commercial people. Eta and Hinin were placed outside of the Tokugawa status system and treated as outcastes. In addition, each stratum was further subdivided. While membership in the above social strata was rigidly determined by birth ascription, so that mobility across strata rarely occurred, the one exception took place during the Tokugawa Period when some Hinin, consisting of vagabonds, beggars, prostitutes, and castoff commoners, were permitted to return to the status of citizens, that is, the status of farmers, artisans, and commercial people. They were regarded neither as "untouchable," as were Eta, nor as hopelessly polluted. As contrasted with Hinin, no mobility was allowed for Eta who engaged in the "polluted" occupational specializations described above.

But generally status discrimination became much more severe with regard to Eta and Hinin than in the previous periods. Feudal rulers issued orders that Eta must wear more humble clothes than farmers, identifying them by rectangular pieces of cloth five by four inches attached to their clothes. When approaching the home of a commoner, Eta were required to take off their headgear and footwear before entering the courtyard. Sitting, eating, and smoking in company of the commoners were also denied to them. In the eighteenth century, citizenship records of Eta and Hinin were filed separately from the others. Often Eta were not generally included in the census. Coins used by Eta and Hinin were not touched by commoners without first being washed, as they were supposedly contaminated with the pollution of the outcastes.

Thus, for the first time in their history, Eta and Hinin legally became outcastes in the Tokugawa Period. Prejudice and discrimination against them intensified as the Tokugawa status system fettered people and their lives more and more strictly. This situation reached its height toward the end of the Tokugawa and early Meiji Period.

The commoners avoided direct contact with the outcastes. The most generally accepted argument concerning the origin of the belief that outcastes in Japan are polluted is in that of Buddhism and Shintoism, which hold certain values, attitudes, and conduct. In Shintoism, there is a belief that the flesh of animals is unclean and displeasing to the gods. Causes of uncleanliness were also related to disease, wounds, death, and all kinds of related activities. This belief was established around the eighth century when the avoidance of contamination was emphasized. Meanwhile, the Buddhist teaching which emphasized compassion to all beings had prohibited the killing of any form of animal life. Thus, in the seventh and eighth centuries, Buddhist emperors issued three official orders forbidding the slaughter and eating of animals. The fusion of the Shintoist and Buddhist notions contributed to the development of the concept of untouchability and encouraged the relegation to outcaste status of those engaged in tasks dealing with blood, death, and dirt.

As has been seen, occupation is a central factor by which the Burakumin were distinguished although there are other equally important factors such as birth ascription of a caste status which contributed to discrimination. Many of these factors are derivatives from occupation. The concept of pollution, for example, is an appropriate case illustrating an association between Burakumin occupations and the belief of contamination.

Hence the Burakumin is not a racial group that carries the stigma of color and other physical features. They are Japanese historically discriminated and given an outcaste status. Here is a distinct contrast between the nature of prejudice against Burakumin and that against Negroes or other racial minorities in America carrying the stigma of color.

Development of Emancipation Movements

The formation of Suiheisha (Levellers' Movement) by the Burakumin in 1922 marks the demarcation between the pre-Suiheisha movement for emancipation and the post-Suiheisha movement.

The most conspicuous characteristic of the pre-Suiheisha movement lies in the fact that liberal politicians and aristocrats, inspired to some extent by Western thought, took the initiative in the attempt to achieve emancipation of Burakumin. A systematically organized, self-directed commitment to the liberation of Burakumin was not seen until 1902. In 1914, about 100 Burakumin in Okayama prefecture organized to protest discrimination in the army (Fujitani 1954: 166–67). The Burakumin riots which had occurred prior to this time had been spontaneous and were not intended to deliberately resolve discrimination and prejudice.

In the period from the beginning of the Meiji Period to 1871, more than half a dozen petitions and recommendations to legally emancipate Burakumin were submitted to the Emperor of Meiji by liberal politicians and government officials who desired to break through traditional shackles to modernize Japan.

In the face of the rising demand of liberals desiring to abolish the Eta-Hinin status, the Meiji government issued Edict Number 61, which states: "The name of Eta and Hinin is abolished. From now both their status and occupation are as equal as the commoners' .... Eta-Hinin's citizenship records are incorporated into the general citizenship records...." The legal emancipation, nevertheless, remained nominal since the Edict was not enforced in any substantial way.

Nonetheless, farmers rioted against abolition of the Eta-Hinin status. Within the ten-year period following the inception of the Meiji Period, there occurred 200 incidents, so called "Eta Seibatsu" (Eta extermination).

By the late nineteenth and early twentieth centuries, however, concern for Burakumin had grown among progressive thinkers, writers and social reformers. In the 1880's and 90's, for example, several books on the study of Eta were published. Similarly, in the 1910's, famous novels and critiques treating Burakumin and their life were written, among which Tōson Shimazaki's *Hakai* was notable. The emancipation of Burakumin was strongly supported by noted social reformers such as Chōmin Nakae and his follower, Sanyu Maeda.

Encouraged by the concern of the social reformers in the Meiji

Period, Burakumin themselves began to initiate attempts to achieve equality. In 1902, for the first time in the history of Burakumin, a self-improvement association called Bisaku Heiminkai was organized by young men in Okayama prefecture under the leadership of Iheiji Miyoshi. Miyoshi believed that the first step in reducing discrimination would be to improve the morale in Burakumin communities having a high incidence of delinquency and social disorder. Although his efforts were specifically directed toward "a movement of spiritual reformation," Bisaku Heiminkai was a significant precursor of the later development of Burakumin emancipation movements.

Meanwhile, with the particular intention of fostering "patriotism" and enlightening Burakumin, the national and prefectural governments started to organize rehabilitation programs about 1905. The programs pointed to the Yūwa (conciliation) movement in the 1910's aimed at the alleviation of Burakumin hostilities against the government. It was developed further with the establishment of conciliatory Burakumin organizations.

Burakumin were not altogether satisfied with such efforts, however, and beginning in 1914 they began to organize self-directed, more aggressive projects against local and national governments. A relevant incident was a Burakumin protest in Okayama prefecture against discrimination toward Burakumin soldiers – a common occurrence when soldiers on a training field sleep in farmers' houses. Burakumin soldiers were refused quarters.

Burakumin's participation in a nation-wide rice riot of 1918 was shocking to the national government. Extremely strained by the unprecedented rise of food prices Burakumin joined actively in the riot, with subsequent wholesale arrests of over 8,000 persons (Fujitani 1954: 171).

Thus far we have reviewed the early steps toward emancipation before the establishment of Suiheisha. Two major interrelated factors contributed to the formation of its actual organization. The first was the growth of a self-directed movement for emancipation developed by radical Burakumin leaders who were opposed to the Yūwa movement. The latter, it will be remembered, emphasized conciliation to fundamental government policies. Aside from the protests and the rice riot mentioned above, there was a formation of anti-Yūwa organizations such as Tesshin Dōshikai (Iron-Mind Comrade Association) organized by Otoichi Ueda and motivated by an incident in which he felt policemen had discriminated against him. Burakumin radicals involved in anti-Yūwa organizations concluded that the emancipation of Burakumin would be achieved through independently organized efforts.

The other major factor was the development of socialism and its subsequent impact upon radical Burakumin. By 1920 Marxism had penetrated the ideological orientations of Japanese progressivists. The most significant direction given to anti-Yūwa leaders was an article entitled "Emancipation Theory for Burakumin" written in 1921 by a leading socialist, Manabu Sano. According to his theory, Burakumin emancipation must be achieved through the struggles of Burakumin themselves organized with solidarity, ultimately developing in a socialist revolution. Their mission was to achieve the revolution by uniting with the laborers' class which suffered from capitalist exploitation. Furthermore, Seiichiro Sakamoto, Kisaku Komai, and Mankichi Saikō, later organizers of Suiheisha, sought emancipation theories from leading theorists of the Socialist League established in 1920.

Finally, the cherished dream of the Burakumin progressivists became concrete in 1922 when Suiheisha was inaugurated under the leadership of Mankichi Saikō, a Buddhist priest. This was the first national Burakumin organization based on progressive orientations aimed at the complete liberation of the discriminated Japanese. Suiheisha adopted three fundamental policies: 1) the attainment of complete emancipation by Burakumin's own action; 2) the demand of economic and occupational freedom; and 3) the continuous march toward a full realization of human values and human dignity.

Between its inception in 1922 to 1940, until it was disbanded under the pressure of militarism, the Suiheisha movement may be divided into three developmental phases.

The first phase (1922–25) is characterized by "thorough denunciation," an eye-for-an-eye retaliation against the discriminating majority as the prime object of the Suiheisha movement, although "thorough denunciation" continued to be less characteristically one of the major activities in the later stages. Denunciation was not always completed by formal apology and repentance by prejudiced persons. It often occurred in the face of a resolute, retaliative Burakumin's demand for apology in public and entailed incidents in which blood was shed when the insulting person did not repent sincerely. The number of cases "thoroughly denounced" during this stage reportedly reached over 3,000.

While denunciation continued, the second phase (1926–31) emerged. Burakumin Marxists insisted on class struggles universal to all proletarians. This contributed to the split of Suiheisha. But later Suiheisha's primary objective, after its reintegration in 1930, was determined to be an "economic struggle" for equal share in economic processes. The primary means of this struggle were generally school boycott, nonpayment of taxes, and withdrawal from government or public organizations such as the fire organization.

The third phase (1932–40) emerged in the eleventh national conference of Suiheisha. The central attention of the conference focused on modifying extremes of class struggles and status struggles. Class struggles ignored the particularity of Burakumin as outcastes deprived of non-Burakumin status, whereas status struggles neglected the universal values and interests shared by both Burakumin and non-Burakumin proletarians. As the direction of the emancipation movement, a synthesis of the two was emphasized. During this stage, however, thorough denunciation and anti-Yūwa struggles were stressed in practice despite, or perhaps because of, increasing suppression of radicalism by the government.

Both the national government and Burakumin conciliatory groups regarded the growing movement of Suiheisha as a serious problem threatening national peace and creating a distance between Burakumin and other people. Consequently the national government provided national funds toward the objective of ameliorating Burakumin communities and other assistance including job rehabilitation and industrial development. The Yūwa movement of this type continued throughout the 1930's.

Finally Suiheisha was disbanded in 1940 under military dictatorship.

Postwar Emancipation Movement

Shortly after the war, in 1946, Buraku Kaihō Zenkoku Iinkai (Burakumin Emancipation National Committee) was organized by Senator Jiichirō Matsumoto, the foremost leader in the history of Burakumin emancipation since the inception of Suiheisha, together with others who contributed to the development of Suiheisha. This was the time when the new Japanese constitution was promulgated prohibiting discrimination of citizens on the grounds of race, sex, religion, belief, or other cultural differences.

The major task of Buraku Kaihō Zenkoku Iinkai, as stated, was to correct extreme personal denunciation of discriminatory non-Burakumin practiced during the Suiheisha period and, therefore, to locate the struggle of Burakumin on the "front of democratic liberation of all people." According to this Burakumin organization, "thorough denunciation" caused a phobia – a feeling of terror – on the part of non-Burakumin toward Burakumin which tended to alienate Burakumin from the majority of the society. Thus, the focal attention of the organization's activities was shifted from denunciation to struggles to improve living conditions, a common concern of many non-Burakumin people as well.

Buraku Kaihō Zenkoku Iinkai was transformed into Burakumin Kaihōdōmei (Burakumin Emancipation League) in 1955. Since that time, Kaihōdōmei has been one of the central forces of cultural change in Burakumin's struggles for liberation.

The foundations of Kaihōdōmei's struggles were crystallized about 1957. For the first time in the postwar period, an officially close relationship of Kaihōdōmei with both the Socialist and Communist Parties began to be built through the formulation of strategies for Burakumin liberation incorporated into Socialist and Communist Party policies. This rapport brought about closer cooperation between Kaihōdōmei, on the one hand, and labor unions and farmer's unions, on the other, needed by Kaihōdōmei to focus upon collective struggles for common goals.

Kaihōdōmei's platform states that the basic cause of discrimination is inherent in the capitalist system of economic production and in the political forms prevailing at present. Political militancy to change them through class struggles is particularly emphasized. At the practical level, struggles are focused upon what is called Gyōsei Tōsō (administration struggle) – struggles to improve living and secure the realization of citizens' rights. Gyōsei Tōsō is developed through imposing Burakumin's demands upon administrators at both the local and national levels. Some of its items are:

– To "acquire through fight" higher living standards;
– To "demand" the abolition of Burakumin unemployment;
– To "acquire through fight" economic aid, medical aid, and educational aid;
– To "demand" the establishment and the improvement of housing, roads, running water systems, sanitation systems, infirmary, bathhouse, playgrounds for children, etc.

Kaihōdōmei encourages Burakumin youth and women to organize into groups for activities through which they share their anxieties, concerns, and hopes, e.g., marriage, love affairs, employment, higher education, in order to develop the ability to attack their problems. Kaihōdōmei emphasizes that it must foster courage and confidence in Burakumin youth to fight against discrimination through systematic guidance. Thus, for this purpose, it demands that local administrative agents of cities and prefectures provide facilities for reading, sports, recreation, and circle activities. It also stresses the development of Dōwa education in schools and social education. Meanwhile the method of denunciation continued to be used, though less frequently.

The organizational structure of Kaihōdōmei has a nation-wide network, with headquarters in Osaka at the national level. At the local level, on the other hand, there are prefectural chapters under whose direction municipal or town branches are organized.

Another Burakumin organization called Nippon Dōwakai was organized in 1959 as an anti-Kaihōdōnmei force. It is a postwar Yūwa group with its national organization directed from headquarters in Tokyo. Organizationally Dōwakai is considerably smaller and less active than Kaihōdōmei. It denies entirely the Marxian principle of "class struggle" upon which the Kaihōdōmei's organizational activities are based. It contends that "class struggle" not only splits the entire nation but also Burakumin themselves. Thus, what is needed is a "spiritual relationship" among people – spiritual solidarity upon which efforts to reduce discrimination and prejudice become effective. In order to achieve the emancipation of Burakumin, Dōwakai argues that cooperation with the present system of local and national governments is essential.

From Dōwakai's point of view, prejudice against Burakumin is inherent in the perpetuating practice of "conventional attitudes" on the part of the majority of the society. For the dissolution of prejudice and discrimination, the first condition is improvement of the social and economic status of Burakumin and their living environment. According to Dōwakai, prejudice and discrimination are associated with lower socio-economic conditions; the elevation of these conditions may lead to the reduction of prejudice and discrimination.

Dōwakai cooperates with the national government in developing governmental policies for Burakumin improvement including the development of industry, the improvement of cultural facilities such as a community center and education. At the same time, it urges the development of Keimō Katsudō (enlightenment activities) through which both Burakumin and non-Burakumin are enlightened toward the abolition of prejudice and discrimination with regard to marriage, employment, education, housing, and social association. In the enlightenment activities, Dōwa education is also included as a part of formal education.

CHAPTER THREE

THE BURAKUMIN IN JUNAN

The city surrounding Junan, a discriminated Burakumin community is Eizen-shi (city). Established as a new municipality in 1954, it is the smallest among five cities in Kagada-ken (prefecture) located 50 miles or less from the capital of the prefecture. The present population of 34,000 has been stable for the past ten years. Every year, four or five thousand people migrate from Eizen into other cities and prefectures, but this is offset by an equal number coming into the city.

The history of Eizen can be traced back as far as the eighth century or even further. Kūho, founder of the Magon sect of Buddhism, was born in Eizen in the eighth century. Having returned from China, he built the main temple of the Magon sect and 49 attached temples within the precinct of two and a half square miles which, accordingly, became the center of the temple town. He named the main temple Eizen after his father's priesthood title. Since then, the town has been known as Eizen. Priests and pilgrims throughout Japan visited this Mecca of the Magon sect for grand ceremonies, festivals, meetings, religious dialogues, and training. With the establishment of the temple, the town became prosperous as Monzenmachi (town of temples). Seven centuries later, the temple was burned twice during battles and the precinct became devastated. Reconstruction to make the temple prosperous again took 30 years. The central pagoda symbolizing Eizen still towers high and pilgrims visiting the temple are seen around the precinct every day. However, the prosperity of the temple is no longer evident. The precinct has become smaller and many attached temples were liquidated. But the commercial district, which developed around the temple precinct, still exists as the shopping center of Eizen. In the district, small inns for pilgrims stand almost side by side.

Eizen-shi is divided roughly ino two major geographical areas, the commercial and the agricultural. The town of Eizen, the commercial area, constitutes the center of Eizen-shi. The integrated villages for the most part compose the farming area, but about 150 manufacturing and processing factories are scattered within these two areas.

The pattern of population distribution within the primary, secondary, and tertiary industries reflects the prefectural pattern to a large extent. The dominant occupation is agriculture, as is typical in non-industrial prefectures. The agricultural population including children and retired farmers constitute nearly half of the entire population of Eizen. In terms of the entire households in the city (a little over 10,000), however, agricultural households comprise less than 30 per cent. Major activities of farmers are the growing of rice and wheat which is grown in rice paddies after the rice is harvested. Because the area of rice paddies per household is as small as one and a half acres, 64 per cent of the farmers are engaged in part-time jobs.

Somewhat more than 3,000 persons are engaged in secondary industries – processing factories and manufacturing. Among these, the largest are food production, comprising 38 per cent; carpentry, 19 per cent; and textile processing, 12.5 per cent. About 4,000 persons are involved in tertiary industries, 65 per cent in retail business and 37 per cent in "service business" such as hotel and entertainment. The Japan Defence Force in Eizen, with its 2,500 soldiers, supplies many of the customers to service businesses. The branch has been in Eizen since 1950, when the Japan Defence Force was first organized.

In the prefecture of Kagada, 444,000 people out of the entire prefectural population of 919,000 are engaged in productive activities. A total of 41.8 per cent are engaged in primary industry. Among these, 90 per cent are farmers and the rest are largely fishermen. The proportion in primary industry has been higher than the national distribution by over 10 per cent in the past ten years. Secondary industry comprises 21.8 per cent at the prefectural level, while at the national level it is 29.1 per cent. The prefectural proportion indicates a four per cent increase in the past ten years. Those engaged in tertiary industry in Kagada comprise 36.4 per cent, 1.5 per cent below the national average. This implies an increase of 10 per cent in the past ten years. As seen above, productive activities in Kagada prefecture are characterized by the domination of primary industry, particularly agriculture, although the distribution of population has been steadily declining.

The largest concentration of Burakumin within Eizen is in the Junan community whose inhabitants are discriminated Japanese, with the exception of 50 or so wives (non-Burakumin) of these people and one family who migrated recently into the community. The second largest concentration is in the community of Kotani, less than half the size of Junan. Several dozen of these Japanese pariahs are scattered in three other communities.

Social Encounter of Burakumin

Nearly a century after the Meiji emancipation edict was issued, Burakumin are still looked down upon and physically and socially discriminated against by the non-Burakumin society although discrimination takes on more subtle and implicit forms than before. Let Burakumin speak to the world they encounter.

At the time of our initial contact with Burakumin in Junan, a man in the early 50's said, they do not know why they are segregated or how they are different from others except for the fact that Burakumin work at "dirty jobs" since they are not able to get more decent ones. Discrimination against Burakumin, he continued, becomes particularly obvious with respect to occupation and marriage. Even a socially important man like Councilman Notsu, a Junan Burakumin, he added, would not ask a non-Burakumin to marry his daughter.

On a cold day in winter, Matsuda, a handsome young man in Junan was married, through the procedure of common-law marriage, to a beautiful barber who was a non-Burakumin and he took her to his home as his wife. The next afternoon, her parents came to Matsuda's home with a policeman. Denying the validity of marriage with a Burakumin, they wanted to take her back to their home. If she refused, they said, the policeman would arrest her since she had not yet reached the legal age for marriage without parental consent. Thus, she was forcibly taken home by her parents under the protection of the policeman to a town 10 miles from Junan. She was confined in her parents' home for a few days, surrounded by the parents and relatives. Meanwhile, Matsuda asked his brother-in-law to visit her parents and persuade them to change their mind. Being adamant, the father refused to talk to him. To encourage his wife, Matsuda, through a student from her town attending a nearby school, smuggled a note to her reading, "Whatever happens, I will be waiting for you." Soon afterward, she made up her mind. Pretending to go to the toilet, she jumped out of a small window and walked to a railway station on her bare feet on the cold, snowy ground to take a train to Eizen. Realizing that her parents would soon come back to Eizen to look for her, Matsuda took her to his aunt's home in a neighboring prefecture where she stayed for two months until she reached legal age. While hiding, Matsuda's "wife" managed to write a letter to her parents telling them she had a job in Osaka, where the letter was forwarded through Matsuda's aunt.

Related to this experience is the suicide of a non-Burakumin druggist which occurred during the time of the research. A young Junan Burakumin had fallen in love with the druggist's daughter and they married despite his persistent objection. Having felt "ashamed" of his daughter's marriage, he chose to commit suicide rather than to suffer the "shame." A part of the note he left, according to Shiroyama, a teacher informant of Yonami Elementary School, read: "I can no longer associate with my relatives and neighbors." This note significantly reveals the attitude of the informants involved in this study toward marriage with Burakumin. All expressed concern that their relatives and neighbors – e.g. the non-Burakumin world – would not accept marriage should their son or daughter marry a Burakumin. There are strong unwritten family and social sanctions against intermarriage.

Another relevant case was described by Kaihōdōmei Prefectural Executive Yoshino and his associate when they invited us to a town 20 miles from Eizen that contains a ghetto of Burakumin when a traditional fall festival was being held. Several weeks prior to the festival a beauty contest was held and won by a Burakumin girl who, incidentally, had not yet been known as a pariah by townsmen. Soon after that contest, she received several marriage proposals but they were immediately withdrawn when her identity was discovered.

As to occupational discrimination, the 15-year-old son of a Burakumin went to Nagoya to work in a factory after his graduation from junior high school. But before a year had lapsed, he returned to Junan because of "strong prejudice against him." He then applied for a job at a public placement office in Shiromachi-shi, about 10 miles from Eizen. After inquiring into his personal background, according to the boy's father, the placement official told him there was no job for him despite the fact that, according to the father's belief, jobs were available there. After this incident, the boy twice failed to get a job due to what his father judged to be "discrimination." His third attempt succeeded and he was employed as a bus conductor near Eizen.

Occupational discrimination was further evidenced by a non-Burakumin, an informant of the research team. An executive of the largest local bank with many branches in Kagada-ken, he admitted that his bank does not employ any Burakumin applicant regardless of his ability. The background of the applicant is carefully investigated not only in terms of his school records but also of his residence and family – occupations and social statuses of his parents and close relatives. This method of investigation, incidentally, is not unusual among the majority of business establishments in Japan. Should this bank employ a Burakumin, this, the banker believed, would cause a protest from other employees as well as patrons. Referring to intermarriage, he said that to imagine his young daughter married to a minority member would be to think of her married to a leper. He stressed that his class – upper socio-economic – should never mix with pariahs although some of the lower class farmers and fishermen do not seem to care about mixing.

One more case which was told by one of the young Junan women at a meeting with us will be considered. At present this woman works in a nearby electric company supplying electricity in Eizen and its vicinity. The company, she claims, employed her without knowing her background. Later her identity, however, was sought out and when her relatives applied for jobs in the company, its president refused to employ them.

Occupational discrimination is more evident when one examines the employment situation in the Junan community. In fact there is only one person holding a stable public service position in the entire community of Junan.

The experiences reported here portray the kind of world where Burakumin live but all Burakumin do not have such direct discriminatory experiences perhaps because they dare not challenge the discriminating world. Conflicting information was offered by both Burakumin and non-Burakumin on the nature of discrimination and prejudice against Burakumin. Nonetheless, both Burakumin and non-Burakumin admitted concertedly that indissolvable discrimination against the former in marriage is an undebatable, explicit fact.

Regarding discrimination in employment, opinions are not unanimous: a P.T.A. Burakumin informant, formerly an active Kaihōdōmei member in Junan told us that discrimination against Burakumin youth in employment has decreased recently. As an example, he referred to his two sons who succeeded in getting "stable jobs" (laundry) from which steady income comes. The fact that Burakumin youth tend to change their jobs, he pointed out, is not due to discrimination but rather due to the lack of their endurance (Ganbari) and due to parents' encouragement that they quit jobs if too difficult. A guidance teacher at Tōzai Junior High School reported that since labor power of junior high school graduates has been highly demanded in the past ten years, discriminatory employment has been avoided to a significant extent. Nevertheless, he detected implicit prejudice against Burakumin graduates. Employers investigate school records, personal characteristics, and family backgrounds. They tend to avoid Burakumin students for the reason that the latter are not "consistent and industrious enough."

Residential discrimination is perhaps more prevalent and overt than occupational discrimination. Half a dozen Burakumin communities in Kagada, in addition to a few delapidated ones in Kyoto which we observed during our research, are segregated ghettos where non-Burakumin families are rarely mixed. (Born and grown up in Japan, the author has seen many other similar ghettos.) The Junan community which will receive more attention soon is one of these.

Finally one brief comment will be made on educational preparation of Burakumin students entering a larger world after graduation. As will be discussed later, more than four-fifths of Junan students terminate formal education at the end of the ninth year (end of compulsory education) while only less than one-fifth of non-Burakumin students do so. Consequently the range of the Junan citizens' alternatives in employment is seriously limited as compared to other Japanese, if considered from the point of view of academic preparation.

Ecological Aspects of Junan

Junan is located on a river bank, as are many other discriminated Burakumin ghettos. On one side, a 200-foot-wide river separates Junan from other communities; on the other, Junan is bordered by a rice paddy separating it from nearby farming communities. At first glance, Junan appears to be entirely isolated from other communities. The fact is, however, that neighboring farming communities give a similar impression to outsiders. One hundred fifty households congregate in a distorted rectangular strip 1000 feet long and 400 feet wide. Furthermore, this dense strip contains a cemetery where Burakumin are buried and an unused crematory; two large junk yards and a garbage yard; a public bathhouse; a public center; a small shrine; a glove factory operated by the city; a small uncovered ditch where various sorts of waste are thrown, and many narrower ditches; many six-foot-wide paths running diagonally to each other; and tiny vegetable gardens.

Outsiders may quickly notice that most Burakumin houses are not only smaller but also shabbier than the average house in Eizen. Many houses do not stand straight but rather lean at various degrees. Our fact survey provides the following comparative data regarding the building site per house and Tatami area (One Tatami is equivalent to 3.3 square meters) per person in Junan and Eizen as a whole.

TABLE I

AREA OF BUILDING SITE PER HOUSE IN JUNAN AND EIZEN

	Less Than 10 Tsubo*	11–30 Tsubo	51–100 Tsubo	More Than 100 Tsubo
Junan	30%	40%	15%	1%
Eizen	1%	23%	19%	30%

* One Tsubo is equivalent to two Tatami area.

TABLE II

TATAMI AREA PER PERSON IN A HOUSE

	1–2 Tatami Area	2–4 Tatami Area	5–9 Tatami Area
Junan	7%	50%	24%
Eizen	1%	23%	40%

As seen in the above tables, the building site per house and Tatami area per person are much smaller in Junan than in Eizen as a whole. In Junan, 50 per cent of the houses have only two rooms and 60 per cent of the total households have between four and six family members each.

Between six and seven hundred people are presently residing in this small area. It is impossible to determine the exact number of the Junan population because it is always in flux. While Burakumin who are former Junan residents, relatives, and newcomers such as common-law wives move into the Junan community without official registration, other Burakumin move out for new jobs, again without making official reports. This reflects a high degree of instability in productive activities of Burakumin in contrast to the stability of non-Burakumin. The aforementioned common-law wives totalling about 50 are non-Burakumin girls who have settled in Junan with their male partners as husbands. Many of them fell in love with Burakumin young men after meeting them in bars, Geisha inns, dance halls, and other entertainment areas. Their ties with parents and relatives, as they explained, have been cut off for a varying period of time until the parents loosen up their resistance against their daughters' unapproved intermarriages. Sometimes communication between them is resumed when second or third grandchildren toward whom most grandparents have deep affection are born.

The high degree of mobility suggests that the practice of primogeniture is less prevalent in the Junan community than in the communities of its vicinity (cf. Singleton 1967: 9–11). According to Okano, a Burakumin P.T.A. informant, unlike the situation in neighboring non-Burakumin communities the first sons in Junan do not necessarily remain home to look after their parents because there is no substantial property to inherit except shabby homes of parents, upon which first sons can make a living. By and large, so told Okano, sons and daughters cooperate to help their parents who depend particularly upon the income of their children since parents do not have a stable source of income.

This, however, should not give the impression that primogeniture is non-existent. It is certainly practiced by relatively richer families such as Councilman Notsu's. He inherited his house and land from his parents whose ancestors can be traced back for a few generations in Junan. His first son attends a big private university in Tokyo. Incidentally, he is one of the two college students from the Junan ghetto.

Speaking of the family, one more unique characteristic is that Junan interpersonal relations are based upon a highly endogamous structure: people in Junan are extensively webbed through kinship systems. For example, Councilman Notsu's household, according to his estimate, is related to about 30 per cent of the Junan families; another family, 20 per cent; one more family, 15 per cent.

The establishment of Junan goes back to the late Tokugawa Period. It originally specialized in leather artisanship such as tanning and drum making. About ten households were congregated on the riverside in the mid-nineteenth century. Since then, expanding gradually, the number of households reached about 40 by 1930. Expansion continued with the result that 100 households representing two-thirds of the present households settled soon after the Second World War. In the past 20 years, about 50 to 60 have been added. A significant phenomenon here is that the population of Junan is still increasing, while in neighboring agricultural communities it is decreasing. According to

Okano, Junan is, in a sense, a "refuge" where Burakumin who left their jobs in big cities for one reason or another – perhaps discriminatory treatment – constantly return to seek help, easy living, or social escape. In fact, he said, living costs are low in Junan, as one can borrow food and other living commodities from others. In addition, people are kind to each other. Junan thus provides protective social conditions to those who, in the view of non-Burakumin people, have not succeeded.

Pattern of Maintenance Systems in Junan

Most conspicuous is the fact that only a small portion of the people in Junan have relatively stable jobs. The majority are jobless and consequently are either on the government economic aid program or the government unemployment program or on both. The contrast between their pattern of productive activities and that of Eizen as a whole is great indeed.

Approximately 70 per cent of the total 150 households are recipients of economic aid which covers expenses for living, housing, medical treatment, education, and a few other items. The amount of aid varies widely depending on the income of the recipient. As an example, a family consisting of mother, father, and two children having virtually no income, due to sickness, receive about $ 50 per month, equivalent to a beginning public school teacher's salary, as well as medical aid.

We were privileged to look into confidential records on welfare files at the Municipal Department of Social Welfare of Eizen. One of the files randomly sampled describes the misery and sadness of a Junan family suffering from economic deprivation, family breakdown, and sad illnesses. Murata, the head of this family, was a peddling shoe repairer covering four or five prefectures whereas his wife was a part-time worker at a small glove factory operated by the municipal government established in Junan to provide work to people in the community. When she applied for governmental relief, she had to support three children and her mother-in-law with a meager monthly income of $ 15 – $ 5 from her work and $ 10 sent by her husband. She often complained not only about her husband's little contribution to the family income but also his long absence. Meanwhile, she was constantly feuding with her mother-in-law. As their welfare file reads, she was always frustrated and extremely restless and apprehensive. This was worsened by a series of unfortunate illnesses: death of her first son caused by diphtheria, development of her heart disease, eye disease of her third son, and sickness of her mother-in-law. When she was hospitalized, Murata returned to seek a job in Eizen. Later he met with an unfortunate traffic accident. Her several attempts at divorce did not succeed since her friends and relatives persuaded her against it at the last moment. She succeeded, however, in separating her mother-in-law from her family. At present she lives with her injured husband and two sons on the welfare income of $ 50 per month from the municipal office. But the medical cost covered by the welfare program is more than twice as large as this income.

One-third of the entire aid appropriated to Eizen citizens goes to Junan. As compared with the proportion of recipients in Junan, the recipients outside Junan constitute six per cent of the entire population. In addition to this program, there is an unemployment program called Shittai (a governmental program for the unemployed) provided to jobless men and women who are healthy and willing to work. Under this program, they are engaged in public construction projects and many other types of unskilled work related to the public service, such as cleaning ditches. They receive a daily wage from the city office. Sixty Burakumin in Junan are presently under this program, more than double the number of Shittai employees in Junan in 1960.

There are two junk dealers for whom about 15 men (and occasionally women) work. Junk collecting fluctuates according to market demand and weather. By and large, the junk enterprise is presently declining, as evidenced by the fact that more than two-thirds of the 45 junk collectors in 1960 have transferred to other jobs. Eight people are engaged in leather work, whereas in 1960 there were about 30. Three people run small food stores. At present, only four people are specialized peddlers selling, for example, cosmetics; in 1960, itinerant peddling involved about 50 men and women full and part time. Fifteen women are engaged in glove manufacturing in the aforementioned factory. In addition, there are six farmers, with one person holding a public-service position in the Yonami Agricultural Co-operative. While those involved in junk collecting and itinerant peddling have declined, the recipients of economic aid under both the economic and unemployment programs have been steadily increasing.

Despite constant conflicts characteristic of the Junan Burakumin community, the most effective system of integrating people is Jichikai, a self-governing association. As in the case of other cities and towns, Eizen has a Jichikai system whose structure and function are more or less similar to other Jichikai systems. Junan Jichikai is one of many Jichikai units in Yonami, one of the towns in the municipality of Eizen. Its primary role is to facilitate maximum participation in grassroots affairs of the community. Thus, when people in Junan, for example, expressed the need for a playground for children, the problem was first discussed in each Kumi, where grassroots people participated directly. The Kumi leader, accordingly, gave a report of the grass-roots discussion to a meeting of all the Kumi leaders of Junan Jichikai, who, in turn, submitted petitions to the respective councilmen of their own communities. Junan Jichikai consists of seven Kumi. Its role will be further considered later in connection with community conflicts.

The important organizations for the emancipation of Burakumin from discrimination and prejudice are Kaihōdōmei and Dōwakai. Most members of Kaihōdōmei in Junan are supporters of either the Socialist or Communist Parties among whom there are officially affiliated Socialists and Communists. An exception is supporters of the Liberal Democratic Party, the ruling conservative party. As contrasted to the ideological constellation revealed by members of Kaihōdōmei, the Dōwakai reflects the ideology of the Liberal Democratic Party. The majority of the Dōwakai members are supporters of the conservative party. In terms of the power relationship between the two organizations, it is almost impossible to determine which is more influential in Junan because of conflicting information provided by Kaihōdōmei and Dōwakai members. For example, one of the informants affiliated with Kaidōhōmei estimated that the number of Kaihōdōmei affiliates who support the Socialist and Communist Parties is three times as large as that of Dōwakai affiliates who support the Liberal Democratic Party. A Dōwakai informant, on the other hand, denied this estimate. The former, nevertheless, admitted the influential power of Councilman Notsu, who, as chairman of Dōwakai in Kagada-ken, has at the same time exerted his influence in building counter-power against Kaihōdōmei. There are, in fact, constant conflicts between the two organizations.

At the same time, there is one more piece of evidence to support the Dōwakai informant's point. Four Kumi leaders of the seven in Junan Jichikai are represented by Dōwakai, whereas three are represented by Kaihōdōmei. Because the chairman of Junan Jichikai is one of the three Kumi leaders represented by Kaihōdōmei, this fact may offset the four-to-three power relationship.

Another important political force is Jirō (All-Japan Free Labor Union), which is the national union of unemployed workers. The majority of the workers on the governmental program for the unemployed (Shittai) in Junan are affiliated with the Eizen local chapter of Jirō, which enrolls some 150 of the total 169 Shittai workers in Eizen. According to Okano, this chapter was originally organized under the leadership of Kaihōdōmei about 1958. It is, he said, now split into two factions due to ideological conflicts. The majority faction is controlled by the Kaihōdōmei, while the minority faction, consisting of about ten members, is influenced by Dōwakai. The present chairman of Eizen Jirō is a Burakumin Communist residing outside of Junan. Within Junan, Katō, one of the most influential Communist members, is active in organizing Jirō members. Fifteen households affiliated with the Communist Party in Eizen are the primary source of Communist influence in the community, while Jirō serves as another important source commanded by these Communists.

Personality

How does the non-Burakumin society look at Burakumin? It is the opinion of most non-Burakumin as well as Burakumin informants in Eizen that the Burakumin personality pattern is different from that of the non-Burakumin. The former epitomized personality characteristics of the Burakumin in Eizen from their personal observations. As perceived by non-Burakumin, the following are traits of behavior and attitudes of the average Burakumin which tend to make them distinguishable:

- Militant, violent, defiant, threatening, frustrated;
- Group-minded, politically oriented;
- Rude, crude;
- Erratic, suspicious, temperamental;
- Less assiduous, wasteful, parasitic, negligent, irresponsible;
- Inconsistent, planless, lack of endurance;
- Hypersensitive, affectionate, loyal.

Several comments made by informants on the Burakumin personality pattern will be selected for consideration.

The most distinctive characteristic of Burakumin behavior, in the opinion of the informants, is the Burakumin's militancy. Non-Burakumin people are "fearful" (Osoroshii) about Burakumin, according to one informant, because of their aggressiveness. "Thorough denunciation" of discriminating non-Burakumin was adopted as the prime objective of the Suiheisha movement as discussed earlier and has contributed to the development of the notion that Burakumin are "fearful." This involved punishment of people who used insulting words, such as Eta, or who revealed discriminatory attitudes against Burakumin. Many bloody incidents have occurred due to adamant Burakumin retaliation against discriminating treatment and due to non-Burakumin's resistance.

One illustration of the militancy of Burakumin involving Junan people is an incident in which 80 Burakumin surrounded the mayor of Eizen for several hours to protest his policies. As arguments between the two parties intensified, according to Ōta, director of the Social Education Department in Eizen who saw the situation, the Burakumin became more and more provocative. Confronting the mayor, they swore at him with such words as "You will be killed," "Go to hell," "Son of a bitch." The mayor finally called the police and could move out of his office only with their help. The militancy of Burakumin is also evident in the schools. At Tōzai Junior High School, which Junan students attend, Burakumin parents are militant and dominate P.T.A. meetings according to Vice President Hashimoto of that school.

In P.T.A. meetings where several active Burakumin parents control decision making, the faculty and P.T.A. members tend to be passive and to acquiesce in the domination of the Burakumin parents who constitute only five per cent of the entire P.T.A. group of Tōzai Junior High School. The following anecdotes provided by informants illustrate the militancy of Burakumin parents.

In one case the decision of the majority of parents and faculty members was reversed by Burakumin parents. The original decision was to buy desks from a P.T.A. fund, but a minority of Burakumin parents insisted upon reversing it. Consequently, it was said that the majority conceded to the minority for fear they might cause further trouble. Another case involved the resignation of a former principal. According to custom, third-year students went on Shūgaku Ryokō (a trip for learning) for three days to see Kyoto and Osaka. One of the Burakumin girls died of acute pneumonia three days after the group returned from the trip. Burakumin parents, backed up by Communist Councilman Ōe (a medical doctor practicing pediatric medicine in Junan as well as elsewhere), one of the key men in the dynamics of Junan, though himself not a Burakumin, protested that the girl's death was due to the negligence of teachers. Accusing the principal, they demanded his resignation. The principal and the teachers defended themselves, pleading that the death of the girl was not due to their negligence. The principal, however, was forced to resign.

The notion that people in Junan are fearful also prevails among children. Yokota, a junior high school informant, was told by his senior friends when he was in the sixth grade, not to associate with students from Junan after he entered Tōzai Junior High School because they were "violent and fearful." Yet he did not know of the existence of the Burakumin until it was discussed by his friend in an interview with the author. According to Sutō, a teacher informant, this attitude prevails to a certain degree among higher grade children at Yonami Elementary School, which also enrolls Burakumin pupils. According to Shiroyama, another teacher informant, the children's perception that Junan children argue and are "violent" is formed by their exposure to frequent fights involving the latter. He contended that aggressiveness of the Burakumin children is a reflection of their parents' militant behavior.

A conspicuous example of militant action of Burakumin is seen in their approach. They have a tendency to organize into groups when they "thoroughly denounce" people they accuse of discriminating. As a few informants commented, however, their behavior and attitude in a group are different from their behavior and attitude as individuals. In a group they are aggressive and crude; individually they are not so to any appreciable degree and are, in fact, even perceived at times to be "good" and "kind."

It has been observed that the Burakumin appreciate affection. As Ōta told us, when they are treated with kindness they never forget. For example, when the most militant Communist in Junan came to the city hall with Jirō members to make protests, they were never violent in their behavior or in verbal expressions toward Ōta, even though they behaved badly toward others. He believed this was because they felt indebted to him for his kindness. He also pointed out that once a relationship of trust is established, they become obedient. He mentioned further that Burakumin are kind, and this observation was supported by non-Burakumin women married to Burakumin in Junan.

Burakumin in general are also regarded as being planless. One informant observed that they place more emphasis on "today" than "tomorrow." According to another informant, this is due to feelings of hopelessness in life and to distrust of the society which discriminates against them in the struggles to attain equal opportunities in marriage and employment. Thus, even though they earn much less income than the average non-Burakumin, they tend to spend it in bars and various sorts of entertainment more frequently than the latter. Their attitude toward work and other matters of social life is also said to be erratic and undisciplined. One informant described them as "parasitic" since most of them do not work seriously to earn a living themselves. He quoted one "industrious" Burakumin shoemaker saying that Burakumin cannot expect emancipation unless they assume an industrious attitude to pave their own economic way toward improvement. A successful Burakumin slipper maker whose small factory is near Junan concurred with the shoemaker and offered a remark without defense: one big problem of Junan people in general is the lack of consistency and responsibility.

Born in Junan and regarded as an influential Kaihōdōmei member Slipper Maker Hikino compared his employees: Non-Burakumin are more responsible and disciplined in work than Burakumin and the former thus are more preferable. While several Burakumin have relatively stable jobs providing constant income, the majority are out of jobs. The latter claim that the fundamental problem is discrimination in employment.

Conflict in Junan

Junan is a dynamic ghetto. It is a community of frustrated people evidenced by their encounter with the discriminating world. It is also a community feared and shunned by the outside world. Yet it is a live, active community with a deep desire for Burakumin emancipation.

Conflicts in Junan tend to be created by competitive struggles for leadership in the community. The most heated recent intra-community conflict was generated by an ideological struggle between the Kaihōdōmei and the Dōwakai members. First a brief mention will be made of local activities of Kaihōdōmei and Dōwakai since they are active factors of the conflict.

Both of these organizations are run by men who have deep indigenous roots in Junan. Two full-time executives run the prefectural office of Kaihōdōmei, one of whom, Yoshino, a Junan resident until recently, served as an informant on our research team. According to him, of a total of 52 Burakumin communities 19 local branches of Kagada Kaihōdōmei have thus far been organized in the prefecture, and 12 more branches are being organized. There are presently about 300 official memberships of Kagada Prefectural Kaihōdōmei. One of

Yoshino's major efforts is to establish local branches in all Burakumin communities and to increase membership by encouraging sympathizers to affiliate officially with Kaihōdōmei. It is Yoshino's hope to achieve a membership of 1,000 within a few years.

Yoshino and his colleague travel a great deal from one community to another. His activities vary widely: negotiations with local administrators for the improvement of community facilities such as a community center, negotiations with city officials and officials of placement offices for the employment and economic aid of Burakumin, obtaining budgets for Burakumin communities, guidance of local branches, denunciation of discriminatory incidents, and negotiations with prefectural administrators to obtain funds for his organization. One of his tangible funds for achievement has been success in helping local branches to employ an additional 42 Shittai workers and 40 people in public programs such as truck drivers' training. A number of these activities and programs involve Junan in one way or another.

Kagada Dōwakai does not have a prefectural office nor a full-time executive of the Dōwakai organization. Councilman Notsu, previously referred to as a Junan resident and the organizer of Kagada Dōwakai, serves as chairman on a part-time basis in his home in addition to his work as a councilman in Eizen. The number of members at the prefectural level is as yet not known. Not available is information on prefectural organizational activities. Nonetheless Notsu's Dōwakai organization is becoming a threat to Kaihōdōmei. As an example, Dōwakai power became dominant in a Burakumin community in Shinju-shi next to Eizen due to Notsu's influence reportedly exerted through his relatives residing there. His influence, however, is far greater in Junan than elsewhere and has become a crucial factor in the dynamics of Junan interpersonal relations.

A comment made by Nose, an active member of Buraku Mondai Kenkyūsho (The Institute for the Study of Burakumin Problems) in Kyoto may well epitomize the two positions of Kaihōdōmei and Dōwakai. Nose said that within Burakumin communities there are class conflicts between "conservatives" – relatively wealthy Burakumin and their sympathizers – and "radicals," i.e. proletarian-oriented Burakumin. The former is represented by Dōwakai and the latter, by Kaihōdōmei.

Differences between the two organizations were revealed at the last prefectural meetings of Kaihōdōmei and Dōwakai held at the time of the senatorial election. At the Kaihōdōmei meeting held in the capital of Kagada, a Socialist Party candidate and a Communist Party candidate were invited to deliver election speeches for one hour in support of Kaihōdōmei. At the Dōwakai meeting held in Eizen, although no Liberal Democratic Party candidate appeared, the invited political figures included the National Chairman of Dōwakai (a Representative in the Lower House affiliated with the Liberal Democratic Party), a Senator, Speaker of the Prefectural Assembly, and other influential political figures of the Liberal Democratic Party.

Notsu and the invited guests spoke about their political platforms and appealed to the audience to support the Liberal Democratic Party. They referred only sporadically to Burakumin problems in connection with the policy of the conservative party. Their speeches took the entire morning session. The audience at the Dōwakai meeting was extremely quiet and orderly and Notsu's relatives were alert so as to carry out the program smoothly.

Meanwhile the participants at the Kaihōdōmei meeting were quite vocal. After the election speeches, the first Kaihōdōmei item on the agenda discussed was the election of executive officers and chairman. A conflict arose among several local branches and the meeting became chaotic. Members of the audience exchanged hot arguments and the chairman lost control of the meeting. Trying to recover his command, the chairman shouted down the emotionally aroused antagonists but he did not succeed. Meanwhile Junan representatives regarded as the most radical group and showing hostility toward other groups, left the meeting hall. At this time, the chairman declared a recess in the hope of persuading them to stay.

After quiet had been restored, a Kaihōdōmei executive, Yoshino's colleague, gave a report of Kaihōdōmei activities and future strategies. Among the many items he discussed were "struggles" against policies of municipal and prefectural governments, denunciation of discriminatory cases, cooperation with Jirō and Seikatsu to Kenkō o Mamoru Kai (The Association for the Protection of Health and Living), a Communist-supported organization, protest against the Vietnam war and the visit of an American nuclear submarine.

Kaihōdōmei's attacks upon Dōwakai and Dōwakai's counter-attacks were repeatedly mentioned by persons on both sides. Kaihōdōmei charged Dōwakai members with "splitting" Burakumin unity by creating an anti-Kaihōdōmei organization. In its view, Dōwakai is simply a puppet organization under the control of the conservative government's Yūwa policy of conciliation. Therefore, Dōwakai, whose many leaders seceded from Kaihōdōmei must be "shattered" in order to restore Burakumin unity and achieve emancipation.

Meanwhile, Dōwakai headed by Notsu countercharged Kaihōdōmei with inciting Burakumin to a power struggle against the ruling class. The former argued that emancipation could be achieved only through good will and the spiritual solidarity of people.

Conflicts between Kaihōdōmei and Dōwakai began six or seven years ago when Councilman Notsu seceded from Kaihōdōmei. Prior to that time he had been prefectural chairman of the organization. His defection, according to several members, was motivated by the following incident, about which conflicting interpretations are still offered.

As described by Kaihōdōmei members, he was publicly accused of absconding with funds Kaihōdōmei had collected for its periodical. Publication was suspended after the first issue, and Notsu was severely criticized over the matter. Hikino, a Socialist and one of the foremost fighters in the organization whom the reader was acquainted with as a slipper maker, denounced Notsu as a "traitor" in printed papers folded into newspapers and delivered all over Kagada-ken. In the face of strong antagonism from some members, Notsu finally not only resigned from the chairmanship but also withdrew from the organization.

Hostility did not cease with his withdrawal, but rather was intensified because he created a new organization, Dōwakai of which he has been prefectural chairman since its inception. Hostilities between Kaihōdōmei and Dōwakai reached their climax when a public bathhouse was built in Eizen several years ago. Feelings of people in the community were intense.

One of the strategies of Kaihōdōmei, as mentioned previously, was to petition the city hall to build a public bathhouse as part of governmental policies for the improvement of Burakumin ghettos. On the other hand, since Dōwakai Chairman Notsu is a councilman of the city, he was close enough to the mayor to gain support for the bathhouse project. Kaihōdōmei and Dōwakai were in total disagreement over the issue of the building site. Through various tactics, they attempted to influence the city hall and take credit for the project themselves.

When the time came to celebrate the completion of the bathhouse, the mood was not one for a banquet because Kaihōdōmei were picketing in front of the newly built bathhouse. By the time the mayor and vice-mayor arrived at the banquet by official car, the situation had become chaotic. Kaihōdōmei's hostility was directed not only against Dōwakai but also against city officials who cooperated with Dōwakai.

As the guests entered the bathhouse, the vice-mayor was pushed by the crowd of Kaihōdōmei members. The banquet was never held. Protesting against Kaihōdōmei's bellicose action, Councilman Notsu requested that city hall be responsible for the operation of the bathhouse and that it be closed by official order. His motivation, according to members of Kaihōdōmei, was a desire to gain credit for the construction of this new community facility, a center of social association where most persons spend two or three evenings a week. The scars of this bitter conflict still remain, as often revealed by informants.

Conflicts between Kaihōdōmei and Councilman Notsu are seen as power struggles between the former and the newly formed organization, Dōwakai, since members of the latter support most of Notsu's actions. Since the bathhouse conflict, other incidents have occurred which have widened the breach between the two organizations. Hostilities between the two are so rife and deep that even brothers and sisters and other relatives no longer communicate with one another in some extreme cases if they belong to different organizations. One relevant case which illustrates this conflict is the confession of the secretary of Dōwakai, whose brother is the secretary of Kaihōdōmei. He said that he is entirely isolated from his brothers and relatives affiliated with Kaihōdōmei. Moreover, he felt bitter hostility directed against him by his neighbors because his home is located in the midst of a block of Kaihōdōmei-affiliated houses. He must therefore be cautious even about receiving guests. In fact, because he "might be suspected by his neighbors," he refused our request to visit him.

One underlying factor assisting the growth and solidarity of Dōwakai in Junan is the notion of loyalty. In a traditional moral framework, loyalty implies one's obedience to his superior and the latter, in turn, is responsible for the former. The subordinate enters into the relationship of On with the superior. The concept of On stands for his indebtedness to the latter always ascriptive to the relationship between the former and latter. Councilman Notsu commands loyalty of a large web of his relatives and other subordinates who owe On to him. His social status and political power as councilman, the tradition of his family, his kinship system, and his personal ability are important contributing factors.

Schools are also occasionally involved in the conflict between Dōwakai and Kaihōdōmei. By way of illustration, an incident told to us by Head Teacher Takebe of Yonami Elementary School will be related. A few years ago, the school lent a tape recorder to Dōwakai at its request without asking the purpose of its use. When it was discovered that Dōwakai was using the tape recorder, a group of Kaihōdōmei members came to the school to protest the use of its recorder for political purposes, accusing the school of supporting Dōwakai. Having been told by them to get it back immediately, Takebe went to city hall and walked into a crowd of demonstrating Dōwakai members to tell them to stop using the recorder.

Indirectly related to the conflict, but relevant in terms of the school's involvement, is the disagreement between Kaihōdōmei and Dōwakai with regard to their views toward the school. While the latter have been acquiescent in the educational program at Yonami Elementary School, the former have been openly critical. Especially in the last half of the 1950's, according to Takebe, Kaihōdōmei often demanded that the school deal more effectively with social problems such as discrimination. Furthermore, they complained that guidance programs and teaching methods are no good. To help alleviate the pressure of Kaihōdōmei's criticism and complaints, the principal of Yonami requested the intervention of Burakumin Socialist Hikino who was exceptionally sympathetic toward the teachers.

A recent incident relating to a playground further illustrates the cleavage between the two organizations. As in the case of the bathhouse, the location became the crucial issue and Councilman Notsu was again the central figure in the dispute. The site selected by city hall for the playground was a riverside strip which was being used as a garbage yard. Although the riverside strip is public land, community people in Junan cultivated small pieces of the land to grow vegetables after the war when food was in short supply. For several years, a few people, among whom was Notsu, rented these small strips of land from the cultivators.

Meanwhile, the seven Jichikai leaders took unified action in supporting the playground project, as they had supported the construction of the bathhouse. In their words, the project was an object of "common need beyond ideology." They also agreed with city hall on the location of the playground and the free release of the cultivated land. According to Jichikai leaders, Councilman Notsu drafted a petition urging the speedy construction of the playground and free release of the land. After the petition was circulated to all Jichikai members of both Kaihōdōmei and Dōwakai for their signature, it was returned to the councilman.

The construction did not start immediately. As reported to our research team by city officials and Jichikai leaders, Notsu demanded that city hall reimburse holders of the released land for an amount much larger than the entire cost of the playground. His argument was that the cultivators had the right to be compensated even though the land belongs to the public. The mayor insisted, nevertheless, that there is no justification for any payment for release of public land since it belongs to the state in the first place. The dispute delayed construction for more than half a year. It was finally begun when city hall decided to make partial reimbursement to the cultivators.

Jichikai leaders affiliated with Kaihōdōmei informed us that they suspected Notsu might have rewritten the petition after it had been signed by all of the Jichikai members. Otherwise, he could not have demanded compensation. Because the land was largely rented by Notsu and a few other Dōwakai members, we were told that he took this action for his own benefit. On the other hand, Dōwakai members, including Jichikai leaders who until this time had supported the original petition, remained silent when Notsu changed his mind.

Despite Kaihōdōmei's charges, Notsu told us that it was he who should be accorded full credit for persuading the city council to vote for the playground project. Furthermore, he pleaded that it was plausible to demand compensation since the cultivators had a "de facto" right to use the land. All in all, this dispute has further widened the breach between the two organizations. The slogan, "common need beyond ideology" of which the Burakumin Jichikai leaders often spoke, did not yield the unity among community people.

Beneath these conflicts between Kaihōdōmei and Dōwakai, there is a political undercurrent centering around Councilman Ōe, the single Communist politician in the city council, who serves as the most influential source of the brain" trust" for the radical unions to which we referred earlier: Jirō and Seikatsu to Kenkō o Mamoru Kai, an organization of which left-wing affiliates of Jirō as well as Kaihōdōmei are also members. While serving as city councilman, he also has a medical practice in Junan. He is responsible for signing many medical certificates necessary for patients in Junan. According to informants hostile to him, however, his frequent visits to the community are not only for medical purposes, but also for instilling Communist doctrines and tactic into the minds of people or for informing them of current issues at the local and national levels.

Through these patients and the organizations in the community more or less under his control, his influence penetrates to a great extent throughout Junan. This was proved in the last election of councilmen.

Ōe, although not a Burakumin himself, received more votes in Junan than did Notsu. As they are mutual foes, opposing each other at many points, their mutual antagonism was manifested, according to a Junan informant, in "indescribable" acrimony in their attempt to destroy each other during the election campaign. This could symbolize the acrid conflict between Kaihōdōmei and Dōwakai.

Unity or Continuing Conflict in Junan

In the first meeting between one of the seven Kumi groups and our research team, a Kumi leader commented that one of the saddest features of the community is that people have been split into two opposing groups – Kaihōdōmei and Dōwakai – at a time when unified action is needed to attack the common problem of discrimination. This is not his concern alone but also the concern of many others, as revealed by other Jichikai members. It is also apparent from Kaihōdōmei Executive Yoshino's comment that the conflicts between Kaihōdōmei and Dōwakai simply paralyze the community. Neither of these organizations has offered an "ideological concession." They adhere to their own doctrines and strategies for change. Nevertheless, as reflected among Jichikai leaders and grass-roots people, their attitude is not entirely pessimistic because there are growing alternatives–an approach "beyond ideology".

Despite bitter ideological conflicts, people in Junan have a desire to unite as cooperative members of one community. The "beyond ideology" approach is still the alternative that Jichikai has offered to achieve this goal. Thus, Jichikai people in Junan, said the Kumi leaders, have agreed not to discuss issues related to Kaihōdōmei or Dōwakai in either Kumi or Jichikai meetings. According to them, problems in these meetings must be discussed by the participants as members of the community and not as members of particular organizations. In meetings of Jichikai leaders, no mention of ideological problems has been made in recent years. The chairman of Jichikai (a Kaihōdōmei member) has also expressed his concern to make Jichikai a unifying force.

Another alternative of the "beyond ideology" approach has been to achieve unity among the women. With the help of a leader of the prefectural federation of a women's organization, an attempt was made to unify the women's groups. However, this endeavor has met with little success.

A third alternative of this approach, still in the formative stages, involves a teacher at Yonomi Elementary School who is now director of Dōwa education at his school. The idea is to integrate people in the community through education, since education, as Burakumin parents put it, is "super-ideological" and therefore the concern of all people. The teacher involved is Shiroyama who, before he came to Yonami, had been teaching with his wife in a small school in an island fishing village. He not only taught the pupils but also helped community people to "improve human relations." When feuds occurred or when community meetings were held, he was often called to assist as a leader or mediator. As he told us, he succeeded over several years in improving human relations and integrating them better. His achievement was reported widely in newspapers and on nationwide television and radio programs.

Although he has been in contact with people in Junan for only two years, he has been accepted by them and has earned their respect. A dozen of them including a few Kaihōdōmei and several Dōwakai members drop in frequently at his home for drinks and "consultation" on a variety of subjects involving problems of children, economic aid, Jichikai problems, and jobs. Occasionally, he invites them to bars and restaurants in Eizen.

Since he is trusted by parents in Junan to a degree where he may be able to take further initiative, he proposed that they organize the Association to Improve Children in which both Kaihōdōmei and Dōwakai parents will be involved. The purpose, as explained by Shiroyama, is for them to talk freely among themselves about problems of education related to Junan pupils, without allowing their ideological interference to block their avenues of communication. He indicated that the most difficult problem would be to shatter what he terms the "double character" of Burakumin. Although education is said to be "super-ideological" the parents' ideological conflicts actually tend to fracture communication and pervade education in his school.

Thus far, Shiroyama has no intention of moving into Junan to help integrate the community people. Although Burakumin psychology, as he put it, is much more complicated than that of fishermen, he believed it is not impossible to achieve unity in Junan if he puts into it as much time and energy as he did in the island. Nevertheless, the proposed venture seems to him to be a first step toward the improvement of the community.

CHAPTER FOUR

BURAKUMIN AND EDUCATION

The historical background of Burakumin including the development of their outcaste status and their organized struggles for emancipation in the Shōwa Period has been viewed. Junan as the largest ghetto in Eizen has illustrated the life of discriminated Burakumin. Junan remains a dynamic and active community, with a variety of involvement in intra- as well as intergroup conflicts despite the deep suffering of people.

In this chapter responses of formal compulsory education to Burakumin problems will be considered. One of the organized educational efforts to attack prejudice and discrimination widely discussed and tried at the national level is designated as Dōwa education. This chapter will focus on the extent to which two schools accommodating Junan students respond to the needs of Dōwa education.

Schools in Eizen

The postwar school system is practiced uniformly in all prefectures in Japan. There is no variation from this policy in the structure of the Japanese school system in the local communities of Eizen.

In the Eizen school system there are two public nursery schools, eight public two-year kindergartens, eight public elementary schools, one private and two public junior high schools, one private and two public senior high schools, and one private Christian college. Approximately 95 per cent of children between the age of four and six in Eizen go voluntarily to kindergartens. Because the kindergartens, though public, are not compulsory, they charge a tuition of $ 1.10 per month. Yonami Elementary School and Tōzai Junior High School, both of which are outside the Junan Burakumin community, accommodate all Burakumin children in Junan. The enrollment of Burakumin children in Yonami Elementary School constitutes about 80 out of the total school population of 290, or slightly less than 30 per cent. In Tōzai Junior High School approximately 55 Burakumin students constitute only five per cent of the total of 1,070 students. Each school has a special education program: Yonami enrolls eight special children of whom four are Burakumin children while Burakumin at the higher level equally constitute half of the total enrollment of ten students in the Tōzai program. In both programs the percentage of Burakumin enrollment is exceedingly high. Eizen Superintendent of Schools Kurono attributed a high rate of mental retardation among Burakumin to their endogamous practice.

In recent years, 85 per cent of all junior high school graduates in Eizen have gone to senior high schools. In Junan, however, only 10 to 20 per cent of the Burakumin students attend senior high school. Those who do not continue their education work at jobs obtained principally through the public placement office of the city. Half of Junan graduates who discontinue their education, however, do not use the channel of the public placement agent but rather seek the assistance of their relatives or acquaintances of their parents. The typical fields of employment which Burakumin enter are: shoe industry, automobile repair factories, general machine repair factories, ironworks, food stores, meat shops, textile industry, etc. Some Junan graduates stay in their community without employment.

Thirty-eight per cent of senior high school graduates continue their education in college. College education is seldom available to Burakumin students, however.

Finally a note on the personnel of the two schools. At present, there are 11 full-time faculty members at Yonami Elementary School, one part-time faculty member, and two full-time secretaries. The staff of Tōzai Junior High School consists of 40 full-time faculty members, three part-time faculty members, one librarian, and three secretaries. In each school there is a faculty member charged with Dōwa education.

School Program

The curriculum of compulsory education as well as senior high school education is determined exclusively by the Ministry of Education. Educational content, class schedules, and other relevant requirements are prescribed in the course of study and in the guide books provided by the Ministry of Education. In this way, compulsory education is conducted uniformly both in public and private schools throughout Japan. At the senior high school level, there are variations in the curriculum as required by the nature of the school, e.g., commercial, industrial, or general senior high schools. In each category of specialization, however, the Ministry of Education's curriculum requirements are enforced to a large degree.

In compulsory education, four basic areas are prescribed by the Ministry of Education: general curriculum, moral education, special education activities (Tokubetsu Kyōiku Katsudō or Tokkatsu), and general school programs (Gakkō Gyōji). The general curriculum for the elementary school consists of eight subjects: Japanese, social studies, mathematics, natural science, arts, music, physical education, engineering, and home economics. The junior high school level curriculums include the following eight subjects in addition to English: Japanese, social studies, mathematics, natural science, arts, music, physical education, engineering (for boys), and home economics (for girls). At the junior high school, 37 hours per week are the minimum requirement for instruction prescribed in the course of study. At the elementary school level, 35 hours are required for the five grade levels except first grade. "Special education activity" includes "special class activity" at the junior high school level, "special class discussion" at the elementary school level, and club activities. One hour per week is required for these activities and discussion at both levels. Their purpose is to develop an independent, self-directed attitude and sociability through children's spontaneous self-activity. In the "special education activity" as in the home room in America, students discuss problems they encounter in their classrooms such as human relations, their responsibilities for maintaining good classroom atmosphere, and others. At Yonami Elementary School, for example, there are efforts to utilize opportunities of "special class discussion" for communicating to each other problems and hopes of both Burakumin and non-Burakumin.

General school program or Gakkō Gyōji is an extracurricular activity planned uniquely by each individual school. It involves ceremonies, study trips, athletic meetings, speech contests, school festivals, music contests, and other activities.

Junan Students in Schools

It was about fifty years ago that Burakumin Socialist Hikino and his classmate, so Hikino said, were forced to repeat the second grade twice without any "valid" reason except that they were minority members.

That was the time Hikino began to apprehend prejudice against his group. As he grew older, he became more acutely aware of his discriminating environment and he chose to fight whenever he encountered prejudice and discrimination. Surprisingly, he managed to graduate from a senior high school in the prewar Japanese school system, though this was a rare occurrence among Burakumin at that time.

Kaihōdōmei Executive Yoshino (aged about 35) was involved in a bloody fight with a non-Burakumin boy who called him "the square root four," a derogatory term invented by non-Burakumin students but used for Burakumin, while he was a student at a private senior high school. "Four" is pronounced "shi" in Japanese which is the phonetic beginning of "Shi-n Heimin" (new commoners) referring to emancipated Eta. Both boys had once been expelled as a result of faculty action, although Yoshino alone was later reinstated. By that time, everybody in the school knew that Yoshino was a Burakumin and he therefore decided to go to Tokyo.

In another discriminatory incident, a senior high school girl felt that she had been "treated with contempt." During a party for her school friends in her home in Junan, one of her guests confessed that she had been instructed by her mother not to touch any of the "very dirty" food. This incident, according to the girl's mother, motivated her to withdraw completely from school. Now she is acting in Takarazuka Theater, a famous girls' theater in Japan.

A number of anecdotes reported to us illustrate that prejudice against the minority group has also been reflected in education in a variety of ways. But this should not mislead one to conclude that prejudice is always present in explicit forms as it was during the Suiheisha movement; contrariwise it tends to take on covert and subtle facades. Yonami Elementary School will be considered.

In an informal conversation with us at Yonami Elementary School, a cook (a woman aged about 50) for the public-funded school lunch, who is a native of the community of Yonami working at the school for five years offered this comment: she has scarcely noticed segregated groups of Burakumin children since she came to the school. Both Burakumin and non-Burakumin children look friendly toward each other and they "seem to be unaware" of being Burakumin or non-Burakumin. This is a great change when compared to the time of her childhood which was spent at the same school. At that time, discrimination, she said, was quite obvious.

As Teacher Sutō pointed out, non-Burakumin children are often instructed by their parents to be "cautious" not to use invidious expressions against Junan children, nor to engage in fights with them which may involve confrontation with militant minority parents. This particular attitude is reinforced during their socialization and in fact, according to Sutō, it is reflected in interactions with Burakumin children. In his sixth grade class, for example, all children know who comes from Junan and they are cautious toward the latter. The "boss" of the girls in this class is a physically superior and athletic Burakumin to whom non-Burakumin even including a few boys are more obedient than provocative.

According to a sociometric survey conducted by Yonami Elementary School, (1) Burakumin children in five classes out of a total of nine are liked by Burakumin as well as by non-Burakumin classmates no less than non-Burakumin children of average popularity are; (2) a few Burakumin children in two classes seem to enjoy higher popularity supported by both groups than other classmates of average popularity; (3) meanwhile, in two other classes Burakumin's personal preference is expressed exclusively toward themselves on the one hand, and non-Burakumin's preference only toward non-Burakumin.

As far as this sociometric survey is concerned, it does not yield a definite pattern of interaction between the two groups. Nevertheless, we were informed by teachers that upper grade non-Burakumin tend to steer shy of Junan children. Meanwhile, according to Shiroyama, Burakumin children are "unusually" sensitive and apprehensive toward other children. Some upper grade Junan children, but not all, become aware for the first time that they are minority members. They are usually anxious, insecure, suspicious, temperamental, and aggressive – traits commonly shared by their parents. It was Shiroyama's account that the parents' hypersensitivity toward non-Burakumin's attitude and behavior is reflected in a configuration of attitudes of their children.

Types of reactions of ghetto children to their outer world vary but dominant among them is aggressiveness. Over 90 per cent of the fights and the stealing which occurs at the school involve them. Their hostility against the outer world was aptly illustrated by an incident described by Shiroyama. On Sunday about a month ago a group of seven Junan graduates (seventh and eighth grade students) came to the elementary school playground to play. They asked at the school for a large aluminum teapot. A teacher discharging the responsibility of Sunday superintendentship (a common practice in Japanese schools) refused to lend it but later yielded to their demand. They tossed it into the air time and again and hit it with a baseball bat. Later it was returned to the teacher in deplorable condition. In the afternoon of the same day the teacher could not prevent these rebellious boys from swimming in a muddy swimming pool, a part of the school facilities.

As their parents commonly do, ghetto children occasionally unite to confront the outer world. The following is one relevant example. A Burakumin group of six elementary school children and a few junior high school students went to a neighboring elementary school to "fight" two non-Burakumin boys. One boy in the former and the latter two had collided against each other when they were riding bicycles. The Burakumin boy was resentful when these two boys did not apologize to him and they decided to retaliate.

Group solidarity for protection against the outer world is emphasized by adult Burakumin. Similarly, children do not fail to attribute a high value to it. A softball team of Burakumin elementary children seems one of the organized ways of strengthening solidarity. It is called Ninja Gumi – a team of hardship. If a member defects from the team, the penalty rule is to hit him 50 times by a bat. This, said Shiroyama, is an imitation of rules of Burakumin "gans."

Aggressiveness and insecurity were mutually reinforcing factors in another incident described again by Shiroyama. A sixth grade Junan boy asked a fourth grade child to give him a ride on his bicycle to a tourist town about 10 miles away. When the latter refused to offer his assistance, the former threatened him with a knife. Similar incidents also recurred among girls. Several teachers including Shiroyama and Sutō at Yonami attributed the cause of insecurity to what they termed "the feeling of persecution" peculiar to Burakumin suffering from discrimination.

Attention will be turned to Tōzai Junior High School which the graduates of Yonami Elementary School attend. Non-Burakumin parents, school administrators, and teachers interviewed in this study denied the existence of prejudice and discrimination against the minority members within the community of this school. The parent informants, however, admitted that parents do generally feel prejudiced against Burakumin. A typical contention offered by the educational panel of informants was that students do not express prejudice toward Burakumin since most of them do not know the "existence of Burakumin"; many students, they said, have not heard of the term Burakumin. Nevertheless, these informants pointed out concertedly that Tōzai Junior High School is the most explosive school in the city because, in their opinion, Junan students attend.

According to Vice-president Hashimoto of the Tōzai Junior High School P.T.A., the ghetto students "cause a lot of trouble" (Takusan no Mondai o Okosu) involving "so many" incidents of violence. This, she said, motivated a number of parents to transfer their children to other schools. She firmly denied that transfer is a reflection of these parents' prejudice against Burakumin; instead she insisted Burakumin themselves are responsible for transfer. Incidentally, her opinion that Junan students are solely responsible for "many incidents" of violence was not endorsed by a son of another P.T.A. informant. He believed that non-Burakimin students are equally responsible. Meanwhele Principal Kando of Tōzai acknowledged that incidents involving both Burakumin and non-Burakumin have decreased recently.

About 50 students were transferred to schools outside the city of Eizen every year until last year. To effect their transfer, parents had to change the children's formal residence from Eizen to Shiromachi, a city next to Eizen, or other cities where relatives live who, as patrons, would accept parental responsibilities. It is illegal to send children to schools outside of the school district if they have residence in the school district determined by the city. Other parents who could not afford to transfer their children "acquiesced" to the local school situation.

Concerned with this situation, the mayor and the superintendent of schools in Eizen tightened restrictions and appealed to parents to co-operate with them by attacking the problems rather than evading them. Parents were assured that the problems which had long been "a cause of anxiety," not only to parents but also to administrators and teachers, would be prevented. As a result, the school seems to have succeeded recently in preventing the transfer of all but two or three children. Vice-president Hashimoto is an example of one parent who was persuaded by the superintendent not to transfer her child. There are, however, parents who are still "extremely" ambivalent about the tightened policy against transfer.

Adding to the hostile environment against Burakumin discussed above, Burakumin students and a small portion of non-Burakumin students who terminate formal education at the end of the ninth year confront alienation from the majority of senior high school-bound students. While the early level of junior high school education is less formally geared to the preparation for senior high school entrance ex-amination, the higher level is more formally structured toward this preparation (Cf. Singleton 1967: 37–40, 48–49). In fact one to two extra-hours are devoted every day to preparatory drilling at the third year level. Furthermore, students are categorized into different groups according to their ability. Drilling is practiced to such an extent that between 25 to 30 preparatory tests are given to senior high school-bound-students. In this context of preparation-oriented education, ghetto students received not only meager attention from their teachers and classmates, but, as teachers admitted, are also bored and frustrated. Polarization between students caused by the preparatory system, said Vice-president Hashimoto and another P.T.A. informant Takano, becomes wider as graduation nears. No wonder Burakumin students walk out during class hours! No wonder also they are rebellious against authority and aggressive toward non-Burakumin students!

Discussing the examination system and its influence upon the nature of education programs, Principal Kando stated that the criteria for college entrance examinations determine not only educational content of senior high schools and earlier levels of education but also methods of teaching and learning. Senior high school entrance examinations, in turn, influence the basic nature of preparatory education at the junior high school level. The kind of education offered at the elementary school level is affected by the examination pressures imposed upon junior high schools. That the framework of expectations for college entrance examinations determines earlier education to a considerable degree may well be viewed as a general manifestation of the dominance of essentialist-traditionalist orientations in Japanese education. None of the informants interviewed denied Kando's observations. The ideal model aspired to by a large number of teachers and parents is, as related by Kando, to send their children to the best kindergarten in local communities, then to Fuzoku Elementary School, then to Fuzoku Junior High School (both the latter attached to Kagada University located in Takatsu, the capital of Kagada-ken), then to Takatsu Senior High School, which is considered to be the most reliable path in Kagada-ken to Tokyo University. Educators, parents, and students referred to the excellent reputation of Takatsu Senior High School and its highly disciplined preparatory training.

Burakumin students receive the least benefit from this competitive, preparatory system which significantly determines the nature of compulsory education. Nevertheless, no conscious effort has been made to correct the division between job-bound and senior high school-bound students. Even though both Superintendent Kurono and Principal Kando agreed that Zenjin Kyōiku (whole-man education emphasizing character development) should be developed, sessions officially devoted to moral education to "special class activity" are often replaced by drills.

The kinds of incidents discussed earlier involving elementary Burakumin students also occur at the junior high school level perhaps more frequently than at the elementary school. They involve collective revenge, individual fights, stealing, and other misdeeds. Burakumin students were characterized by teachers, school administrators, and non-Burakumin parents as rebellious, aggressive, disturbing, suspicious and frustrated in no less identical way than they were at the elementary level.

One incident reported by Principal Kando will be presented here which may throw some light upon the nature of ghetto students' behavior as characterized above. A group of five second year Burakumin girls approached four non-Burakumin girls to seek their friendship. The former asked the latter to meet at a nearby senior high school in the afternoon on a cold day in December. In response to the request, the latter showed up at the place. Burakumin girls proposed that their leader and one representative of the other group would cut fingers with a blade prepared by Burakumin girls to exchange blood so that friendship might be firmly established. When one non-Burakumin girl, frightened with this proposal, refused to become their friend, she was ordered to undress and show her nakedness. She became further frightened and burst into tears. As a result, the exchange of blood also failed. Burakumin girls then asked the other girls to share the money they possessed to buy candies. The latter hesitantly gave money which totalled 50 cents.

This incident was reported to a councilman by the parents of the non-Burakumin girls who warned in the city council that transfer of students would resume unless the superintendent of schools would prevent further occurrence of similar incidents. Meanwhile the parents of the Burakumin girls "sincerely" apologized to the parents of the other group and the principal when they were told about the incident by the principal.

Junior high school teachers at Tōzai and school administrators involved in the study offered accounts of such incidents claiming that ghetto students are responsible for incidents. Interviewed parents also supported this view. Nevertheless these informants did not fail to tell us that several Burakumin students are intellectually superior and leaders among their classmates. One Burakumin, according to the principal, is an "exemplar" for all second year students. The parents of these Burakumin students, said Principal Kando, are "constructive" and supportive of his policy.

According to Seitokai leaders the faculty of Tōzai Junior High School tends to avoid their involvement in problems related to Burakumin students. The following may reveal their attitude toward Burakumin. A case of Seitokai involvement will be considered.

Seitokai is a students' self-governing organization whose objective is to govern and develop a community of students through self-directed activities. Its central role is to organize the life of the students in the school through club activities, committee activities, and the enforcement of rules. Tōzai Seitokai takes considerable responsibility in maintaining order in the students' community within the school. The Seitokai officers who are elected by the entire body of students and Shūban (student patrol) members are particularly committed to this task. They formulate weekly schedules to improve order in the school community, such as students' attitudes, behavior, and problems of cleaning the building. To enforce Seitokai rules, they patrol the school two or three times a day. Thus, two meetings of the Seitokai officers and Shuban members are held daily, one in the morning and another in the afternoon, to coordinate their roles and to review their observations.

There are two kinds of Shūban members, the school Shūban and the class Shūban. The former consists of 12 members chosen by Seitokai officers on a cross-grade basis from the entire Seitokai membership. The class Shūban group is composed of several members of each class responsible for order in their own classrooms. Both groups work in a close relationship.

Leaders of Tōzai Seitokai have attempted to improve the behavior of rule-breaking students who are rebellious, deviant, violent, and mischievous. Among these students are both Burakumin and non-Burakumin deviants. Special attention will be given to Burakumin students.

The principal and teachers, in the opinion of Seitokai leaders, try to ignore the misbehavior of Junan students because of the militancy of Burakumin parents. Two anecdotes were provided which support the observations of Seitokai leaders. In one case, the principal himself concealed information that he was hit by Burakumin students, although it is reasonable to assume that he would not have concealed the incident if non-Burakumin students had hit him. The head teacher, according to the other anecdote, pretended not to pay attention to Junan students when he saw them smoking on the school campus. Seitokai leaders deplore this cowardice and submissiveness.

Seitokai leaders have reportedly played an aggressive role in coping with problems of deviant and mischievous behavior. When they discover students breaking Seitokai rules, Yamada, president of Seitokai, and other Seitokai leaders issue an admonition immediately or take deviant students to the Seitokai room for further warning so that they will not break Seitokai rules again. As a result of their continuous efforts, misbehavior of both Burakumin and non-Burakumin students has been reported to have decreased considerably. Yamada's charismatic influence seems to have played an important role in these efforts. In fact, deviant students who tend to be rebellious against teachers have become docile to Yamada and a few other Seitokai members. According to a student informant, students show more respect to Yamada than to ordinary teachers because he courageously faces difficulties that they hesitate to tackle. In Seitokai's attempt to change the behavior and attitudes of deviant students, some Burakumin students have built up hostility toward Yamada, and Burakumin graduates have occasionally intimidated him.

Seitokai's aggressiveness is not welcomed by faculty members. On one occasion, Yamada found a student smoking on the campus and took him to the teachers' office for admonition by the principal. Contrary to his expectation, said Yamada, instead of admonishing the Burakumin student, the principal told the Seitokai leader to treat the student more carefully. He further commented that Yamada was too aggressive. Seitokai leaders deplored the "little support and encouragement," as they put it, given by the faculty members in their commitment to improve students' attitudes and behavior at school. Consequently, they resigned from their Seitokai posts but were persuaded by the teachers to continue in their roles as Seitokai leaders.

Yamada, aged 17, who interrupted his education due to illness, became acquainted with the history of Burakumin through books he read. He remarked that he cannot understand why prejudice and discrimination against Burakumin prevail. Meanwhile two other Seitokai leaders attending several meetings with us where Yamada was also present did not hear about the minority group until Yamada referred to it. Neither their parents nor neighbors have mentioned the Burakumin group to them. Among six students of a college in Eizen who offered assistance to our research team, three became acquainted with Burakumin problems recently; three others learned about Burakumin after they entered senior high schools.

While teachers try to avoid involvement in Burakumin problems, Burakumin students and their parents practice mutual avoidance to a degree. As the guidance teacher of Tōzai remarked, about half of Junan graduates do not seek employment through the guidance of their teachers and public placement agents perhaps for fear that they might encounter unpleasant prejudice. Instead, they rely upon their relatives and acquaintances. The guidance teacher did not offer any account for this phenomenon. Usually non-Burakumin students, according to him, seek their jobs through the channel of the public placement agent.

Four Operating Elements in Dōwa Education at Yonami and Tōzai

Dōwa education was previously referred to as an educational attempt to overcome problems of prejudice and discrimination against Burakumin. In reference to Burakumin students, the nature of Dōwa education practiced at Yonami Elementary School and Tōzai Junior High School will be considered here. Conflicts are involved in the development of theory and practice of Dōwa education which will be given attention first. At least four significant elements interplay in the implementation of Dōwa education and determine the degree of continuity between alleged objectives and practice – the explicit and implicit levels of commitment to Dōwa education.

Kaihōdōmei is the most deterministic element in the development of Dōwa education. As discussed elsewhere, since the time of Suiheisha, the progressive elements now constituting Kaihōdōmei have attempted to expose both overt and covert forms of prejudice and discrimination to the public for the purpose of increasing their understanding of Burakumin life. Because they believe that their liberation consists in the resolution of contradictions in the present Japanese socio-cultural systems, they do not hesitate to use any means available to change, expose and scrutinize prejudice and discrimination which, in their view, are all rooted in these contradictions.

They have, therefore, turned to the school as a channel by which to sensitize both Burakumin and non-Burakumin children toward understanding the nature of prejudice. Kaihōdōmei claims that the school should systematically deal with the problems of prejudice and discrimination, for example, through the treatment of Burakumin history and analyses of individual cases of discrimination.

As the second element, Dōwakai takes a negative stand toward Kaihōdōmei's attempt to critically expose children to reality. Although Dōwakai officially contends that Dōwa education must be developed, it offers neither abstract nor practical frameworks. In actuality, its stand may suitably be expressed by a Japanese phrase often used by informants: Neta Ko o Okosuna (Do not wake up the sleeping child), which is equivalent to the English phrase, "sweep under the rug." What is meant by the Japanese phrase in relation to Dōwakai's position is that children should not be exposed to the facts of discrimination. Furthermore, they believe that if children learn the reality of prejudice and discrimination against Burakumin, their awareness may contribute to psychological and physical separation between Burakumin and non-Burakumin children, instead of to harmonious assimilation.

A typical argument used by Dōwakai members is as follows: most elementary and junior high school students scarcely know of the existence of the Burakumin minority group. Therefore, it is not necessary to treat the Burakumin problems at the school unless a concrete case of prejudice arises among the children. They urged the school to put more emphasis on moral education and the development of Burakumin children's academic ability.

The third element is the resistance of many teachers who do not wish to cope with pressures of the two major Burakumin organizations or to become involved in their conflicts. Most teachers are said to have a high degree of anxiety as to whether they are approved by outspoken Burakumin. Particularly in the treatment of Burakumin problems, teachers feel they must be exceedingly cautious not to cause trouble. Many teachers, in fact, tend to be hypersensitive about the alleged militancy and aggressiveness of Burakumin. They therefore attempt to avoid critical treatment of Burakumin problems.

There are two categories of teachers who hesitate to make a commitment to Dōwa education. The first category includes teachers who are willing to develop Dōwa education programs, handling individual problems of prejudice and discrimination as they arise. But they are not confident enough to communicate with and obtain support from Burakumin. The other category consists of teachers who may be ambivalent about Dōwa education. Although they seem to show their concern with Burakumin problems at the explicit level, in practice they refrain from becoming involved in the core of Dōwa education. This ambivalent attitude of teachers may be described by another Japanese phrase used by Principal Kando: "Furenai," meaning "do not touch." The implication of the Furenai attitude is that one can be saved from criticism, severe accusation, and attacks by Burakumin by avoiding involvement in a critical problem. Teachers taking the Furenai attitude seem to assume that Burakumin problems may disappear gradually if serious conflicts with Burakumin are avoided.

The fourth operating element is either the unwillingness of non-Burakumin parents to support Dōwa education or their open resistance to it. As Sutō told us, non-Burakumin parents would not willingly support the Dōwa education program of Yonami Elementary School if it developed systematic programs requiring more commitment and time of teachers. Because they believe that Dōwa education is only for a small minority of children, they demand the school should devote equal attention to problems of the majority of children.

The indifference of many parents toward Dōwa education was evidenced by P.T.A. informants at Tōzai Junior High School. Although admittedly unfamiliar with Dōwa education at Tōzai, they maintained that it is unnecessary because, in their opinion, there is no discrimination at the school. They feared that inculcation of facts and knowledge about Burakumin into the minds of students who do not have the notion of prejudice might produce negative effects on the part of students. Concern for discrimination and prejudice against Burakumin, they contended, might threaten both Burakumin and non-Burakumin students.

Neither students nor most parents are aware of the nature of Dōwa education despite the fact that the Dōwa Education Committee is one of six committees of the Tōzai P.T.A. The Dōwa Education Committee consisting of parents and one faculty advisor are organized for the purpose of developing understanding of Dōwa education and Burakumin problems. They hold one or two lecture meetings on Dōwa education given by outside resource persons and send representatives to national conferences of the National Dowa Education Study Association (Zenkoku Dōwa Kyōiku Kenkyū Kyōgikai or Zendōkyō) as well as to local conferences. The indifference of non-Burakumin parents to Dōwa education at Tōzai is evident in the fact that even Vice-president Hashimoto was hardly acquainted with its program.

The Kagada Dōwa Education Study Association (Kagada Dōwa Kyōiku Kenkyū Kyōgikai or Kadōkyō) rightly points out the cause of the slow progress of Dōwa education in Kagada, namely, the opinion of teachers and parents that is not necessary. It is their belief that: "there is no problem of prejudice"; "it is unnecessary to wake up the sleeping child"; "the present situation is much better than the past"; "there are doubts as to the effectiveness of Dōwa education." Kadōkyō further points out that the practical evidence of this opposition is illustrated by the fact that about 30 or 40 per cent of Burakumin communities and schools accommodating Burakumin children in the entire prefecture of Kagada oppose Dōwa education. In view of this fact, "non-Dōwa schools," that is, schools which do not enroll Burakumin children, Kadōkyō concludes, are hardly aware of the significance of Dōwa education. The four elements discussed here, namely Kaihōdōmei, Dōwakai, teachers' resistance, and parents' indifference, are essential determinants affecting the developments of Dōwa education as will be seen below in greater details.

Dōwa Education at Yonami

Dōwa education at Yonami Elementary School began in 1957 under the guidance of the Prefectural School Board primarily because progressive Burakumin demanded the launching of a Dōwa education program. The teachers, Sutō recalled, were unfamiliar with Dōwa education at that time because they had never been exposed to the treatment of Dōwa problems in an organized way. In 1958 an attempt was made to treat Dōwa problems within the framework of moral education which had just been initiated. In 1959 the previous program was developed somewhat further with the application of a conceptual scheme presented in the 1958 conference of Zendōkyō. This scheme provided a rationale for Dōwa education, according to which prejudice and discrimination might be ultimately dissolved if basic biological, psychological, and social needs such as love, freedom, health, happiness, and economic security were satisfied. To provide objective data for the program, Yonami Elementary School did research covering the evaluation of Burakumin children's academic ability and I.Q., human relations between Burakumin and non-Burakumin children, their desires, their practical judgment, "morality tests," and family environments.

In 1960 the central theme of Dōwa education was the improvement of academic ability based on the rationale that the emancipation of Burakumin – the access to greater opportunities for the satisfaction of needs which are culturally sanctioned – rests primarily upon the higher development of academic ability on the part of Burakumin children. As part of its effort to develop Dōwa education, the faculty of Yonami Elementary School conducted a series of discussions with parents in ten sub-school districts with the support of both Burakumin and non-Burakumin parents in order to increase communication between these parents. The central purpose of the discussions was to talk frankly about their concerns related to Burakumin without fear of being intimidated by Burakumin. These concerns included problems regarding the lack of communication between the two groups as well as socialization processes through which Burakumin children acquired undesirable behavior traits. In order to hold discussions with parents, teachers visited each community in the school district and served as a communications channel between the Burakumin and non-Burakumin parents in conveying their views and observations to each other.

In 1961 the emphasis of Dōwa education was placed on group guidance to make children more sensitive to their daily problems and the realities of life. Contending that crucial problems of Burakumin culture were not treated thus far in the view of radical Burakumin, Kaihōdōmei opposed Dōwa education, while Dōwakai remained silent. Kaihōdōmei urged the school to develop a program based on Zendōkyō orientations by which to sensitize children toward social reality. In order to avoid political involvement, according to Sutō, Yonami Elementary School deliberately developed a moderate program of Dōwa education by disassociating itself from Zendōkyō.

In view of the criticism offered by Kaihōdōmei, the teachers of Yonami worked diligently to develop a more comprehensive program in 1962 and 1963. The program which they designed, however, was not what Kaihōdōmei had envisioned as an effective Dōwa education program. The program will be looked at closely.

Although the program is a specific educational attempt to solve problems which both Burakumin and non-Burakumin face in their mutual encounter it does not have any specific focus upon these chronic problems from which the Burakumin have long suffered. It is inferred, nonetheless, that the basic assumption of Dōwa education upon which the Yonami program was built was to develop a healthy personality in the child, whether Burakumin or not, unfrustrated emotionally and equipped with intelligence. Consequently, this assumption blurred the basic rationale of Dōwa education, that is, the liberation of Burakumin from the slavery of discrimination and prejudice. Under that assumption, accordingly, Yonami Elementary School attempted to improve human relations of children, methods of teaching, and psychological and physiological environments.

Following is the outline of Yonami Dōwa education.

1) Improvement of learning ability. For the purpose of improving

learning ability, the following efforts were planned:

a. Reorganization of the annual educational plan
b. Improvement of educational content
c. Improvement of teaching methods
d. Supplementary tutoring for slow learners
e. Improvement of "home learning" through the encouragement of parents
f. Improvement of communication between teachers and parents by means of "communication notes."

2) Improvement of health education

a. Prevention and treatment of decayed teeth
b. Prevention of myopia
c. Improvement of nutrition
d. Encouragement of sports
e. Improvement of hygiene.

In order to improve these five aspects of health education, the school worked closely with the P.T.A. Health Committee consisting of P.T.A. members.

3) Cultivation of healthy sentiments

a. Morning gatherings of children. On Mondays, all children and teachers gathered in the auditorium. They sang songs. Representatives of the children read memoranda citing good behavior and attitudes of children. They listened to teachers' talks. On Wednesdays, gathering in the playground, all children did "radio gymnastics."
On Fridays, in their classrooms, they listened to poems and compositions written by the children themselves and broadcast throughout the school.
b. At lunch time, records were played.

4) Improvement of the school environment

a. Trees were planted and school gardens were expanded.
b. A new concrete block fence was built.

5) Fostering self-directedness of the child

The central purpose was to encourage the child to think creatively and independently.

6) To foster the notion of equality in the mind of the child specific attention was paid to social studies which deal with concepts of equality and freedom.

7) Publication twice a year of the *Sasayaki*, a 20-page school pamphlet.
   In the *Sasayaki*, children, parents, and teacher expressed their feelings, opinions, and desires as frankly and honestly as possible so that it might help them to communicate better with one another. For example, a second-grade child wrote the following note to her father:

Daddy, you often scold me. Daddy, do you really hate me since I was born? You come back late at night every day, Daddy. Do you know I wait for you to come home. I do not like you to return so late at night. Daddy, please come home earlier.

This composition exemplifies the nature of the *Sasayaki*, which implies "little voice."

8) Improving human relations among children.

In this brief outline of Yonomai Dōwa education, which has been conducted for two years, it can be seen that there is no explicit focus on Burakumin problems. In fact, in the pamphlet describing the above program entitled "We Conduct Dōwa Education This Way," prepared by Yonami Elementary School, no explicit reference was made to Burakumin problems whatsoever, despite the contention of teachers that they paid specific attention to Burakumin children in carrying out the program. However, Sutō confessed, it was exceedingly difficult to deal with Dōwa problems in this type of program covering the whole range of education for the development of personality, and, as a consequence, there is need for the formulation of a focus around which the treatment of Burakumin problems can be programmed.

Reviewing the difficulties of the previous program in 1964, the teachers at Yonami attempted to deal with Burakumin problems within the framework of moral education with a clearer focus and more attention to problems of segregation and prejudice. Thus, they have compiled a guide book intended to treat Burakumin problems in relation to moral education. It is based upon the 36 precepts formulated by the Ministry of Education and describes the relationship between the content of Dōwa education and that of moral education as follows:

The Teaching Content of Dōwa Education	The Content of 36 Moral Precepts
1. To develop the child's ability to look critically at slavery and feudal systems.	International cooperation, peace, and love of mankind.
2. To make the child understand the historical development of human nature and the necessity of the modern society.	Implication with social studies.
3. To make the child understand the history of modernizing process and a future image of an ideal society.	Self-autonomy, justice, courage.
4. To have the child understand institutional systems and movements of the modern society and their purposes.	Freedom and responsibility.
5. To make the child realize that an essential task of Japanese democracy is the resolution of the unemancipated Burakumin, and that it is a national assignment.	Rights and Duties.
6. To have the child think concrete cases which block the development of free man and some possibilities to free man.	Justice, courage, honesty, sincerity, fairness, generosity.
7. To foster the child so that he may express his thoughts and desires.	Self-autonomy, independence, cheerfulness, frankness, idiosyncracy.
8. To build an image of man who respects others and who is sincere.	Progress, hope, effort, frontier spirit, respect of rules.
9. To have the child develop his attitude to cooperate with others.	Neat arrangement.
10. To have the child realize the importance of human life and develop his personal pride as a man.	Contemplation, self-reflection, temperance.
11. To make the child feel it is his duty to develop reason and conscience.	Individual uniqueness.
12. To have the child realize that every man is innately equipped with reason and conscience and to motivate the child to love and respect every human being.	Trust, friendship, kindness, sympathy.
13. To have the child understand discrepancies of our modern society and orient him toward the resolution of problems of discrimination embedded in feudalism and old customs.	
14. To have the child grasp the dichotomies that man is discriminated against due to the differences of status, birth, occupation, economic class, and sex.	Respect for life, health, security.

15. To have the child's understanding of human rights deepen and motivate the child to reject any discrimination. — Respect for personality.
16. To have the child develop the notion of equality and consciousness of his rights.
17. To have the child learn unbiased facts on Burakumin in the context of history and social movements, and build an attitude to liberate Burakumin. — Implication with social studies.
18. To have the child understand socio-economic conditions that perpetuate Burakumin segregation, and consider an improvement. — Rational spirit, creativity, adventure and inquiry, proper manners, protection of materials, respect of time.
19. To guide the child to adjust to modern society. — Public mind, public morality, love of the school.
20. To have the child learn educational and employment conditions which create discrimination against Burakumin, and consider improvements. — Strong will, endurance, respect for labor.
21. To orient the child toward the effort to dissolve historically determined prejudices by the methods of reason. — Piety, love and protection of animals and plants, respect, gratitude.

The above is an archetype showing the relationship between Dōwa and moral education, according to which a Dōwa education program for each grade was incorporated into moral education. Although there is a clear place for Dōwa education within the framework of moral education as far as the conceptual scheme is concerned, several serious limitations were pointed out by Sutō.

As contended by Sutō, moral education which is given one hour a week is not considered effective at Yonami Elementary School. Consequently, in Sutō's view, this implies that Dōwa education itself is not effective either. In addition, most teachers are extremely cautious in dealing with Dōwa problems. As previously mentioned, they fear a variety of reactions from the hypersensitive Burakumin. Thus, to preclude Burakumin reactions, teachers tend to avoid a critical treatment of the problems of segregation.

Although Kaihōdōmei may be hypersensitive in criticizing moral-Dōwa education, they urged the school to build a more effective and systematic program of Dōwa education. Sutō supported them without hesitation; however, he felt that children are not yet ready to discuss Burakumin problems objectively by using textbooks and other organized materials on prejudice and discrimination. This opinion was based upon his fear that both Burakumin and non-Burakumin children might be considerably "shocked" by learning the facts concerning segregation and discrimination of which they were not previously aware. As children gain some basic knowledge in the area, he hoped to use a textbook dealing with the history of Burakumin and their culture edited by the Tokushima Dōwa Education Study Association.

Shiroyama, director of Dōwa education at Yonami, planned to create two more opportunities to deal effectively with the problems of Burakumin children with minor attention to those of non-Burakumin children. In his view, Dōwa education is concerned not only with problems of prejudice but also with the improvement of Burakumin children's socialization – a process of learning values, concepts, and attitudes, from their own culture and that of others. As pointed out by several teachers, chronic problems such as stealing and fighting at Yonami are often fermented by Burakumin children. Thus, one of the important commitments of Dōwa education, Shiroyama said, is to attack these problems with more effective means which might yield more satisfactory results.

The first opportunity, as previously mentioned, is to organize the Association to Improve Children in which both parents and teachers assume joint responsibility in attacking the problems. The second opportunity is "special class discussion" by which children share mutual responsibility and cooperate with one another in helping themselves to grow. Shiroyama planned to organize it by the end of 1965.

The uniqueness of the first opportunity is the fact that concern for the problem of Burakumin children is shared by teachers and Burakumin parents alike. The purpose of the association is to discuss children's problems and concerns of parents and teachers as frankly and openly as possible. Thus far, because Burakumin parents sometimes tend to conceal their children's problems, there has not been frank communication between parents and teachers or among parents. Shiroyama said the teachers and parents would be in a position to formulate strategies for solving many of their problems when parents must share responsibility in revealing relevant facts and discussing them in mutual cooperation.

The second opportunity is the one whereby children may share their own problems with the guidance of teachers. "Special class discussion" is utilized as an opportunity by which children express their anxieties, frustrations, desires, and opinions with frankness and honesty. Shiroyama emphasized that the atmosphere should be as permissive as possible in order that they may express themselves effectively. Through this communication, Shiroyama hoped that children would understand one another better and would become more cooperative and sympathetic with one another. They will then organize cooperative efforts to improve themselves by making new rules and programs. When giving guidance to children, the teacher will record their discussions so that problems discussed by children may be studied in faculty meetings. Shiroyama further emphasized that if "special class discussion" develops well, it will help both Burakumin and non-Burakumin children to appraise themselves critically and grow further through cooperative interactions. In order to improve "speciall class discussion," Shiroyama planned three meetings during summer vacation in which all teachers at Yonami would be involved in presenting their "special class discussion" problems and programs for discussion and further improvement. It was his hope that the Association to Improve Children and "special class discussion" will contribute to the growth of Burakumin children.

It has been shown that a discrepancy exists between the implicit and explicit levels, as illustrated by Dōwa education at Yonami Elementary School. The purpose of Dōwa education at the school is to resolve prejudice and discrimination against Burakumin by means of systematic teaching and learning. This, however, is simply the explicit objective of Dōwa education. As seen previously, Yonami Elementary School has attempted in various ways to achieve this objective. Nonetheless, the means employed and the content in process were not effective because they were not explicitly intended for implementation of the alleged objective. As a matter of fact, teachers at Yonami have hardly succeeded in treating Burakumin problems systematically in terms of Burakumin history or problems of segregation and prejudice which exist wherever Burakumin exist. Dōwa education, after all, has been conducted for eight years at Yonami without direct involvement of students and teachers in these focal problems.

Dōwa Education at Tōzai

A greater dichotomy is seen at Tōzai Junior High School. According to Superintendent Kurono and Principal Kando, their "most serious concern" has been the problem relating to Burakumin children and their parents. On the one hand, Burakumin students at Tōzai are often seen as juvenile delinquents, trouble makers, and problem children and they are thus said to be responsible for the transfer of non-Burakumin students. On the other hand, Kando and the teachers at Tōzai have been deeply concerned with the militancy of Burakumin P.T.A. members who constitute a little less than five per cent of the whole P.T.A. body. Kurono and Kando said that these parents arbitrarily have dominated P.T.A. activities with aggressiveness which is typified by a communist who attempts to liquidate anything institutionally established at the school.

Despite his alleged concern with Burakumin students, Principal Kando did not think that a systematic Dōwa education program dealing with specific Burakumin problems is necessary because, in his opinion, there is neither segregation of nor prejudice against Burakumin students at the school. Thus, he concluded that moral education, without any specific focus on Burakumin problems, would suffice to cover Dōwa education. He felt that if there is prejudice on the part of non-Burakumin, it is generated by Burakumin's particular attitudes and behavior, namely, militancy, irresponsibility, parasitism, and rudeness. Burakumin children, he said, reflect the value orientation and attitudinal organization of their parents. Therefore, if they relearn attitudes and values acceptable to the majority, there would not be any serious problem of segregation or prejudice. Hence, Kando's formula for the liberation of Burakumin consists largely in their reorientation or resocialization through which they internalize the values of the majority. Interestingly, this view has been supported by two informants who are officials of Eizen School Board: Superintendent Kurono and Social Education Director Ōta. They also agreed with Kando that a Dōwa education program dealing with Burakumin problems specifically is unnecessary in view of the fact that there is no problem of prejudice among students.

According to Kando, about half of the teachers at Tōzai are unwilling to have any Dōwa education, while the other half recognize the importance of such education. Kando categorized himself as one of the latter. He felt that a direct approach to Burakumin problems is dangerous because it can easily arouse sensitive Burakumin to react militantly to teachers and the school. He believed the most feasible approach is an indirect one. It may take the form of general guidance and moral education with no focus upon the treatment of the problem of prejudice. He suggested, for example, various educational opportunities such as moral education, "special class activity" and weekly morning meetings of students in the auditorium. The indirect approach is also acceptable to the majority of P.T.A. members who do not support Dōwa education.

The teachers at Tōzai, however, are not free from conflicts when they maintain the indirect approach. They have been under pressure from

Burakumin parents who urge the school to organize a systematic, direct approach to Burakumin problems. Thus, several representatives of the faculty, along with critical Kaihōdōmei parents, attend annual conferences of "radically oriented" Zendōkyō, local meetings, and demonstrations of Dōwa education.

A further reason why there has been no organized effort at Tōzai to build a Dōwa education program, according to Nose, a teacher informant at Tōzai, is that the teachers in common with Yonami teachers are afraid of becoming involved in the ideological conflicts between Kaihōdōmei and Dōwakai which put conflicting pressures upon the school. Another relevant reason may be the apathy or unwillingness of non-Burakumin parents to support Dōwa education which was also one of the important factors at Yonami. For these reasons, Tōzai has not prepared any materials on Burakumin problems.

The sole effort to develop sensitivity toward Dōwa education is that of the P.T.A. Dōwa Education Committee which involves only active Burakumin parents although its official membership includes both Burakumin and non-Burakumin. This evidence indicates that Tōzai has not been making significant progress in attacking the problems of segregation and prejudice affecting Burakumin. Unlike Yonami, Tōzai has hardly developed even an indirect approach to Dōwa education which might resolve Kando's "most serious concern." Also, there are serious discrepancies in the attitudes of teachers at Tōzai toward Burakumin problems and Dōwa education. Supporting Principal Kando's position, teachers have not paid sufficient attention to the influence of adult values, attitudes, and prejudice against Burakumin upon the socialization of children. Certainly, most adults, admitted various informants, have various degrees of prejudice against Burakumin. For example, Kando also admitted that most non-Burakumin Japanese do not approve of intermarriage between them and Burakumin. It is well known that prejudice of adults is both consciously and unconsciously internalized among children in the process of socialization. Therefore, progressive leaders and Kaihōdōmei members contended that children must understand the nature of Burakumin problems through Burakumin history and the analysis of prevailing prejudice and discrimination, so that the internalization of adults' prejudice will not take place.

A further dichotomy can be illustrated by Kando's conflicting views. At the explicit level, he claimed that the teachers at his school must do their best to attack Burakumin problems, but he himself has avoided the school's commitment to the problems at the implicit level. His "most serious concern," consequently, has not been resolved since he has not yet developed an effective strategy of change with which to attack it.

Kando's extremely cautious effort to avoid conflicts with Burakumin parents is evidenced by a case related to this study. When our research team met Kando for the first time to ask for his permission to study his school in October, 1964, he cordially welcomed us and granted our request. In about a month, we held another meeting to explain the methods of this study, including the selection of informants and the interview technique. We asked him for an opportunity to speak to three bodies of school which include the P.T.A., the student body, the faculty members to explain the study to them. Although he gave us an opportunity to speak to faculty members, he hesitated to let us meet either the students or the P.T.A. for six months. He seemed to feel that if students and P.T.A. members knew of our intention to study Burakumin problems at his school, the parents would militantly protest against his cooperation with our research team. This, in turn, would have created a serious problem at the school. He wished to select student and P.T.A. informants personally lest Burakumin parents should hear of the school's involvement in the study of Burakumin problems. After having experienced a serious conflict with Burakumin in the past, Kando insisted that the most appropriate attitude for the school to adopt is "Buraku Mondai ni Furenai" (not to touch Burakumin problems). Finally persuaded by Superintendent Kurono, he gave our research team permission to speak to members of the student body and the P.T.A. provided that Burakumin problems were not included in the speech.

Vice-president Hashimoto and Parent Takano were aware of the principal's "Furenai" approach to controversial problems. In concurring with the Seitokai (Students Self-governing Organization) leaders, they remarked that the principal and his faculty members had tried to avoid involvement in problematic situations, particularly with regard to problems related to Burakumin students. This tendency is likely to conceal various incidents such as students' violence, juvenile delinquency, and other types of socially disapproved conduct in which not only Burakumin students but also non-Burakumin students are involved. In the view of Hashimoto and Takano, the principal and the teachers at Tōzai are not merely uncommitted but are also anxiety-ridden and acquiescent. Their attitude, therefore, may well be interpreted as "nothing can be done" under the present situation. As the P.T.A. informants contended, they consider their present positions as temporary. Thus, they attempt to evade controversial issues and keep silent until they are safely transferred to another school.

As a related example for the indirect approach to Burakumin problems, Kitano Elementary School in Eizen will be mentioned. It has 28 Burakumin children enrolled, constituting 10 per cent of the pupil population. Dōwa education there, however, does not involve the treatment of Burakumin problems any more than at any other schools in Eizen. Dōwa education, in the view of teachers at Kitano, is not a particular strategy for attacking Burakumin problems alone, but rather a strategy of change by which to free children from prejudice by building "friendly human relations" among all children at the school.

In order to observe classes where Dōwa education was conducted, we attended the Dōwa Education Study meeting for Eizen District sponsored by Kadōkyō and the Prefectural School Board held at Kitano. Teachers at Kitano demonstrated classes where basic problems of human relations were treated, with particular regard to the teachers' conception of Dōwa education. It was found that they were teaching social studies or moral education without any reference to Burakumin problems. Ironically, one teacher was dealing with segregation of American Negroes instead of Burakumin, perhaps because this indirect approach might be safer and less disturbing to students and teachers alike. Here again is a dichotomy in their approach to Dōwa problems. Even though they aim explicitly at the extinction of prejudice against Burakumin, they deliberately avoid the treatment of Burakumin problems. As a consequence, the meaning of Dōwa education is obscured. Unlike Tōzai Junior High School, Kitano Elementary School, however, has made conscious efforts to develop an indirect approach to Dōwa education.

Yano, Vice-president of Kadōkyō, is sympathetic with the Kitano teachers' view. Unlike most teachers and principals, Yano, principal of an Eizen elementary school, is married to a Burakumin woman. Problems of discrimination and prejudice, Yano said, must be treated directly when they occur in relation to children. But he was not yet convinced that it is practical to deal systematically with Burakumin problems. In fact, in his opinion, most teachers are not yet ready because they lack sufficient knowledge of methods for dealing directly with the problems of the Burakumin. According to him, there is no school in Kagada-ken where a systematic approach to Burakumin problems has been organized.

CHAPTER FIVE

NATIONAL POLICIES AND LOCAL RESPONSES

Dōwa education is a difficult, sensitive area for local teachers to implement effectively. There is, as we have seen, a spectrum of teachers' reactions to Dōwa education ranging from the "Furenai" (evading) approach to the search for creative and effective alternatives. What is shared by most teachers in this spectrum of attitudes and reaction patterns is, however, their concerted efforts to avoid conflicts with Burakumin. Such efforts, in turn, have led them to a situation where they are squeezed between radical and conservative Burakumin. The nature of local Dōwa education is influenced by the dynamics of various factors contributing to the conflicts of alternatives, commitments, and interests. Among them significant, it will be remembered, are Kaihōdōmei, Dōwakei, and teachers and administrators.

We shall turn to national policies of Dōwa education and local reactions to such policies. At present, there are two types of Dōwa education based upon two distinctive ideological orientations. One rests, in principle, upon a Kaihōdōmei and Socialist-oriented ideology, the other on a conservative orientation. The former is basically determined or guided by Zendōkyō (National Dōwa Education Study Association), a voluntary national association of schools, whereas the latter is sponsored by the Ministry of Education. Zendōkyō-oriented Dōwa education and government-supported Dōwa education are often in conflict due to their radically different ideological orientations.

Background of Zendōkyō

Zendōkyō was organized in 1953 and it articulated the goals of Dōwa education in the *Guide Lines for Dōwa Education* in 1958. The ultimate goal of Zendōkyō is the complete emancipation of Burakumin as well as other "discriminated" and "culturally deprived" people in Japanese society: "To foster a person who is emancipated from all discrimination is true democratic education. We call the education which centers in the commitment to the emancipation Dōwa education" (Zendōkyō 1964: 173). Zendōkyō (1964: 175) states further:

Dōwa education is not a special education which consists in a special program of educational activities. It is nothing but democratic education founded on the demands and needs of citizens suffering from discrimination; education which attempts to arrive at truth, rooted in the reality of people's tasks. Providing a basic principle of education, it modifies education and serves as a criterion by which to determine curriculum and educational materials. Therefore, Dōwa education must be viewed in terms of the whole program of educational activities.

In order to fulfill its goal, Dōwa education, as stated in the guide lines, attempts to sensitize children toward the reality of prejudice and discrimination as well as toward those socio-economic conditions which generate that reality. According to Zendōkyō, it is particularly essential to foster children's understanding of the discrimination against Burakumin based upon socioeconomic class, family tradition occupation, sex, and locality, which reveals itself in restricted educational opportunities, a narrow selection of occupations, restricted marriage, segregated housing and social associations, and economic deprivations. In short, it aims at developing children's critical attitudes toward the cultural order that generates prejudice. At the same time, the commitment required of Dōwa education is, more positively, to develop a fundamental desire among children for liberating the segregated. Zendōkyō emphasizes the improvement of the academic ability of Burakumin children as a path toward emancipation because it is an intellectual tool by which to implement goals. Dōwa education, Zendōkyō contends further, is not only for Burakumin and the segregated but also for the nonsegregated. It must be conducted through formal and informal educational programs at schools, community centers, and other means of adult education.

The radical orientation of Zendōkyō took a concrete form at the 11th National Dōwa Education Study Conference held in 1959. Dōwa education was declared to be an educational program directly confronting capitalism because it was believed that discrimination and prejudice were fostered by the capitalist system. This caused negative reactions from moderate members and participants of the conference. They neither understood the practical relationship between Dōwa education and anti-capitalism, nor accepted the Zendōkyō slogan that the objective of Dōwa education was to uproot the present Japanese capitalist system. Among the participants were Kagada teachers who had not yet joined Zendōkyō and they also rejected the Zendōkyō slogan adapted at the conference.

In the background of the Zendōkyō platform one detects a strong overtone of Marxism; that is, a Kaihōdōmei orientation. A typical Kaihōdōmei-oriented view on Dōwa education articulated by Kiyoshi Inoue (1964), a Marxian historian, holds that because Burakumin segregation has been continued under capitalism, Dōwa education should train men who have the will and ability to change the present social order of the capitalist economy. Thus Inoue (1964: 290) argues:

The image of man Dōwa education fosters is the man who, as mentioned previously, is capable of understanding discrepancies and dichotomies of the modern society which retains feudalistic discrimination...; the man who has ability and desire to fight against discrimination and the reactionary, undemocratic order of our society and its politics.

Another influential Marxist interpreter of Burakumin problems is Tarō Ogawa, a pedagogue who has provided a theoretical framework of Dōwa education. Discussing the perspective of Dōwa education, he (1964: 123-24) concludes:

To create truly demoncratic educational opportunities and conditions; to reformulate educational goals and contents to fulfill citizens' hopes; to develop through education the ability to actualize freedom and happiness; to implement education for the citizens – all these are the present task of education for the citizens at this stage of our history. At the same time they are the assignment of Dōwa education. Dōwa education is certainly an education for the discriminated and the poor at the lowest social stratum. And because of this role that Dōwa education plays, it can also represent education for the citizens. Meanwhile it exposes to critical attention the education for powercontrol and discrimination created by monopolistic capitalism.... The masses will begin to understand that present discrimination in general serves monopolistic capitalism as a means of control when they examine critically discriminatory educational opportunities and conditions, and discriminatory educational goals and contents.

When Kaihōdōmei-oriented Dōwa education was initiated after the Second World War, there was considerable involvement of many teachers and children.

Takashi Tōjō (1962: 120-25), another theoretical proponent and popularizer of Dōwa education, explained the development of Dōwa education by dividing it into three stages. Zendōkyō was organized during the first stage from 1945 to 1953. During this period the notion of democracy became a popular concept in education. Guided by the concept of democracy, however, Dōwa education became too abstract. It regarded discrimination and prejudice as merely psychological rather than sociological phenomena. Because its role was understood to cause repentance and guilt feelings on the part of those who segregate Burakumin, Dōwa education became "an extremely spiritualist and moralist type" of education (Tōjō 1962: 120).

During the second stage, from the inception of Zendōkyō in 1953 to the eleventh conference in 1959, an anti-capitalist slogan was adopted. The progress of Dōwa education in this period was accelerated by the support of the Burakumin emancipation movement, which showed remarkable progress during the same period, and by various endeavors of teachers. It was characterized by increased recognition that discrimination and prejudice are not merely psychological but rather are rooted deeply in post-psychic factors, namely, socio-economic conditions. Dōwa education, therefore, was concerned with socio-cultural dimensions such as school drop-outs, health conditions, sanitary conditions, juvenile delinquency, and lack of opportunities for promotion to senior high schools and for employment.

The third stage from 1959 to the present time has been characterized by the development of cross-sectional collaboration among Zendōkyō, Kaihōdōmei, and other organizations involved in the emancipation movement, as well as by the integration of teachers' efforts devoted to the advancement of Dōwa education. Tōjō emphasizes that it is of great significance that the slogan of the Zendōkyō conference clarified the role of Dōwa education. It otherwise contributed to paving the way toward complete separation of Zendōkyō Dōwa Education as a wholly "voluntary movement of education" from Dōwa education supported by the Ministry of Education (Tōjō 1962: 124).

Government-Supported Dōwa Education

Very limited information is available to us regarding government-supported Dōwa education. While information supporting Zendōkyō-oriented Dōwa education is disseminated through publications of a number of books, periodicals, newsletters, and papers, the source of governmental information, as far as we could detect, is limited to official pamphlets.

Governmental Dōwa education was initiated in 1959 as part of the "Ten-Year Plan for Dōwa Strategies"* organized in 1958 and designed

---

* The term Dōwa used here is not associated with the term Dōwakai; it denotes peaceful integration of Burakumin and non-Burakumin. Similarly, Dōwa as used in Dōwa education is not also associated with the term Dōwakai.

by the Cabinet Council for Burakumin Problems (The Ministry of Education: 1965: 101). The central objective of Dōwa education sponsored by the Ministry of Education is not to develop critical attitudes toward the present cultural order but rather to improve human relations and educational conditions under which Burakumin children learn. The Ministry of Education (1965: 96) states:

It is clear in the Japanese Constitution that citizens by virtue of the basic human rights, should not be discriminated against on the ground of race, beliefs, sex, and status. But an evil practice to discriminate against a part of our comrades still remains in our nation. The solution of this problem requires not only the cooperation of all citizens but also the development of the spirit for harmonious integration of all men through school education and social education.

Thus a major role of education, as conceived by the Ministry of Education, is to encourage the assimilation and socialization of segregated children into the nonsegregated population. It is not, however, intended to sensitize children toward dichotomies of the Japanese social order as conceived by Marxist-oriented radicals.

This government viewpoint, it will be remembered, is supported by Dōwakai. The Dōwakai position is traced back to the late Taishō and early Shōwa periods when Suiheisha began to organize resistance against discrimination. Educational efforts devoted to the amelioration of tensions between Burakumin and non-Burakumin as well as discrimination were framed as Yūwa education (education for assimilation). The assumption of Yūwa education was based upon the moral concept. that all people are brothers united in peace (The Ministry of Education 1965: 100). From the point of view of Zendōkyō, however, governmental Dōwa education is still nothing but Yūwa education – a program by which to induce Burakumin to acquiesce to the present social order.

The Ministry of Education (1965: 97) suggests four general guiding "principles" for developing Dōwa education. First, Dōwa education practiced in the framework of formal education ought to be conducted through all domains of educational experience of students including subject matters, moral education, "special educational activities," and other relevant programs. Second and third, Dōwa education should be integrated "harmoniously" into the total programs of the school. Particularly is it essential to introduce Dōwa education gradually according to the developmental readiness of the students. In dealing with Burakumin problems, the teacher must be "particularly cautious." However, when a specific Burakumin problem occurs among students, the teacher should make use of this opportunity to advance Dōwa education by treating the problem as effectively as he can. Fourth, schools are encouraged to study Burakumin situations in their communities to promote teachers' understanding of the reality of Burakumin life.

Zendōkyō Organization and its Role

We attended the 16th Zendōkyō Conference in December, 1964. More than 3,000 representatives and participants from 20 prefectures gathered in a large gymnasium in Ise, Mie Prefecture. They consisted of teachers, school administrators, parents, students, and observers. After the morning general assembly, the representatives and participants were divided into 11 symposiums which continued for three full days. The slogan adopted for the conference was: "Dōwa education for all in which all are engaged; Dōwa education which digs out problems at the grass-roots; Dōwa education which fosters desires and heightens them." As seen here, the slogan of anti-capitalism which characterized Zendōkyō orientation in the late 50's disappeared completely from the 16th Conference. Although this may not imply that Zendōkyō has become conservative, there is an evident shift in Zendōkyō strategy for attacking practical problems.

The most impressive and stimulating aspect of the conference was the series of 11 symposiums which were held in schools and meeting rooms of Ise Shrine. Lively reports and enthusiastic discussions were presented for two days. What impressed us furthermore was the fact that both reporters and participants were deeply involved. The following themes were pursued from the viewpoint of Dōwa education: educational conditions, educational groups, educational contents, guidance for promotion to senior high schools, Kodomokai (children's clubs), infant education, women, youth, activities of community centers, educational administration, and an introduction to Dōwa education for beginning Dōwa educators. This annual conference is central to Zendōkyō programs. It is a single opportunity for all Dōwa programs and problems throughout the nation to be presented and exchanged for critical review and further progress. The preparation for the annual conference is one of the major responsibilities of the Zendōkyō Office.

At present, 18 prefectural associations constitute the Zendōkyō organization in which Kagada is not yet included. Its headquarters is in Kyoto with five full-time staff members, a director, and four junior high school and elementary school teachers. Although the four teachers are employed by several school systems, they engage in the programming of Zendōkyō activities on a full-time basis. There is also the Board of Directors consisting of 16 representatives which meets once a month. In addition, there is the Zendōkyō Committee in which four representatives from each member prefecture serve as committee members. Four meetings a year are held to determine problems and programs of Dōwa education. It is the director's responsibility to call these meetings as well as to edit the *Dōwa Kyōiku*, the Zendōkyō monthly journal and reports of the annual conference. Since the organization is completely independent of the Ministry of Education, all Zendōkyō programs and activities are operated from membership fees and income from publications.

Each prefecture affiliated with Zendōkyō has an association of Dōwa education. Within each prefectural association local branches serve as implementing centers where teachers often meet to develop Dōwa education programs. Although the fundamental direction of Dōwa education is determined by Zendōkyō, the prefectural branches are given a wide range of flexibility to develop programs relevant to their localities. This is an inevitable consequence resulting from the fact that each prefectural branch does not necessarily follow the guidelines formulated by Zendōkyō.

Conflicts between radically motivated and moderate or conservative branches were revealed in the 16th National Conference. By way of illustration, the conflict between the Tokushima branch and other branches such as Kōchi or Kyoto will be pointed out. Being in a conservative prefecture, the Tokushima branch was severely attacked by radical branches due to the fact that the former leaned toward the ideology of the Ministry of Education, deviating from the Zendōkyō framework. As a result of these conflicts, radical elements of Zendōkyō tended to isolate and intimidate moderate members and participants by accusing them of deviation from the central line of Zendōkyō. A relevant example was Zendōkyō's adoption of the 1958 anti-capitalist slogan as the central direction of Dōwa education which was unfortunate because many teachers did not follow Zendōkyō. In view of the negative reactions of the moderates, Zendōkyō has modified its position to a certain degree.

Responses to National Policies

At this point, we might return to the governmental program of Dōwa education. Every year the Ministry of Education selects about 60 elementary and junior high schools in the nation as "project schools" for Dōwa education. It provides these project schools with a very limited amount of financial aid. Yonami Elementary School, which was designated as a project school in 1965 received $ 56 from the Ministry of Education. Kagada prefecture, as a whole, was granted $ 489. The Ministry of Education grants are given to the prefectural school board which is requested by the Ministry of Education to develop Dōwa education in the prefecture.

The responsibility of each project school is to submit a short report on its program to the Ministry of Education. The program is not strictly prescribed by the Ministry of Education but is developed by individual schools within a certain framework suggested by the Ministry of Education. The following examples indicate the variety of Dōwa education programs in project schools in 1964 and 1965: improvement of academic achievement, counseling, moral guidance, improvement of the school atmosphere, improvement of human relations, and guidance for promotion to senior high schools. The theme on which Yonami Elementary School has been working since 1964 is "moral education and Dōwa education." In Kagada prefecture there are only four project schools. Other schools accommodating a large number of Burakumin children receive occasional guidance from the Kagada School Board.

Governmental Dōwa education has been criticized as being too superficial and ineffective, merely giving lipservice to the demands of Burakumin. Teacher Sutō, who served as former director of the Dōwa education program at Yonami, is one of many critics. The governmental Dōwa education projects, he contended, do not have much value since the Ministry of Education provides neither adequate grants nor basic guidance. To develop an effective Dōwa education program in his school, he stressed that a grant should be provided to employ at least one full-time specialist in Dōwa education. The same point was emphasized by an official who is in charge of Kyoto Dōwa education programs under the Kyoto Municipal School Board. Without stronger leadership of the Ministry of Education and stronger financial means of implementation he felt that the governmental programs cannot become effective enough to attack problems of prejudice and discrimination. In his criticism, the director of Zendōkyō Headquarters pointed out the lack of clear theoretical formulations upon which governmental Dōwa education should be built.

There are often conflicts between governmental Dōwa education and Zendōkyō Dōwa education when prefectural school boards and local Zendōkyō branches share no common objectives. Conflicts exist therefore where both are antithetical in their ideological orientations. There are cases, however, which demonstrate cooperation. Kyoto is one example developing such cooperation between the Kyoto Municipal School Board and the Kyoto Zendōkyō branch. An important reason for this cooperation, we were told, is that the former is progressive enough to share the common responsibility for improving Dōwa education.

Kadōkyō (Kagada Dōwa Education Association) is comparable to that of Tokushima Dōwa Education Association which is moderate in its ideological orientation though the former may suffer more from conflicts between the conservative ideology represented by the Prefectural School Board and radicals represented by Kaihōdōmei. On the one hand, Kaihōdōmei exerts pressure to force Kadōkyō to join Zendōkyō and, on the other hand, the Prefectural School Board exerts counter-pressures to maintain Kadōkyō as an organization disassociated from Zendōkyō so as to prevent the influence of the Zendōkyō orientation. Such conflicts might well reflect the fact that both the Prefectural School Board and Kaihōdōmei are polarized. Meanwhile cooperation between the Prefectural School Board and Kaihōdōmei exists in such cases as Dōwa education meetings sponsored by the former. And also in the past, Kadōkyō, although not a member of Zendōkyō, has sent about 40 teacher representatives to Zendōkyō National Conferences every year, 21 representatives attending the 16th Conference in 1964. Also present at the conference were half a dozen Burakumin parents affiliated with Kaihōdōmei and a few prefectural school officials. Every year the Kagada Board of Education contributed funds to cover their expenses. Kagada participants in the conference prepared long conference reports whose copies were distributed among local teachers. Furthermore, local meetings including active Burakumin parents were held to review the implication of the conferences for local concern.

Kadōkyō was organized in 1962. Its formation was a collective response to growing needs for Dōwa education increasingly pressed by Zendōkyō which provided a source of stimulations to local teachers involved in Zendōkyō Conferences including those who were not formally affiliated with Zendōkyō. In fact, Kadōkyō's structure and programs are very similar to those of other Zendōkyō affiliated prefectural chapters. Meanwhile a tangible influence of the Ministry of Education upon the formation of Kadōkyō is not detectable. There is no nation-wide conference organized by the Ministry of Education comparable to the Zendōkyō Conference where several thousand representatives from many prefectures gather to share problems and to seek guidance.

Kadōkyō's membership in 1965 consisted of 70 schools. Looking briefly at its program of 1964, several events are significant. In addition to the national conference, another is the Setomi Dōwa Education Conference held annually, to which Kadōkyō sent its delegates. There were two demonstration study meetings, each of which combined the observation of demonstration classes, discussions, and lectures on Dōwa education. Both of these meetings were co-sponsored by schools and the Prefectural School Board. Two study meetings co-sponsored by the Prefectural School Board were held which aimed at studying Dōwa education programs; two meetings for the training of leadership and three meetings of the Kadōkyō Planning Committee were also organized. The *Dōwa Kyōiku*, the Kadōkyō periodical published three times a year which reports all its activities, serves as an important communication channel between Kadōkyō and the schools. It states the goals of Kadōkyō programs as follows (Kadōkyō 1964: 5): "to deepen the understanding of Burakumin problems; to disseminate valid and practical knowledge concerning Dōwa education; to study contents and methods of Dōwa education from a practical point of view."

According to Kadōkyō President Yano, teachers' interest in and sensitivity toward Dōwa education have been developing slowly from year to year. Thus it is planned that all elementary and junior high schools in the prefecture, regardless of whether Burakumin children are enrolled or not, will be given Kadōkyō membership in the near future. Yano believed that Dōwa education should be given to all children because in his view it is not a special program dealing only with problems of prejudice and segregation but rather is a more comprehensive program by which to attack problems related not only to Burakumin but also to the culturally deprived and underprivileged in general. As has been seen, a large portion of the Kadōkyō program is co-sponsored by the Prefectural School Board, which shares responsibility in developing Dōwa education in Kagada.

Behind the implementation of these programs, whoever the sponsor might be, there have always been pressures by Kaihōdōmei urging schools and local and prefectural school boards to develop strategies and programs by which to attack Burakumin problems. Although ideological positions of Kaihōdōmei and school boards are different, the former demands more involvement of the latter in the developing of Dōwa education. Equally significant is the fact that these pressures have also contributed to the modification of Kadōkyō's original position maintaining its formal dissociation with Zendōkyō to the effect that Kadōkyō leaders have been persuaded to plan their formal association despite the Prefectural School Board's resistance to such formal affiliation.

Meanwhile, being under the supervision of the local and prefectural school boards and the Ministry of Education, local schools espouse policies formulated by them as seen in the case of the Dōwa education project. In view of this fact, Kagada Dōwa education has been developing according to the orientations of both the Ministry of Education and Kaihōdōmei. Local schools respond to these organizations in an ambivalent way as, the reader may recall, in the ambivalent responses of Yonami Elementary School.

CHAPTER SIX

SEARCH AND PERSPECTIVE

Below the average among 50 Burakumin communities in Kagada-ken in terms of socio-economic conditions as estimated by a Burakumin leader, Junan has little shared the unprecedented progress of Japanese economy. Nor has it shared the substantially greater educational opportunities for higher education provided by the postwar educational system which the majority youth now enjoys. No wonder one radical Junanese Burakumin felt that the richer the majority Japanese become the more poverty Burakumin suffer. Junanese recipients of welfare aid have phenomenally increased in the 1960's as many Junanese gave up such jobs traditionally ascribed to Burakumin as peddling, junk collecting, and shoe making in favor of enlisting in the governmental unemployment program.

Meanwhile, we observed that even though discrimination against Burakumin in employment, housing, and marriage is obvious, such discrimination is considered a taboo that should not be discussed publicly nor even privately in a family in the presence of children. Underlying feelings are encapsulated by a frequently used expression "Do not touch a dangerous thing." Consequently, it is likely that many children, adolescents, and even some of those in the early 20's will not be acquainted with the social practice of discrimination against Burakumin until such time as minority members are discussed in connection with marriage. This observation was substantiated by Superintendent Kurono, Principal Kando, Social Education Director Ōta, and others. Furthermore, it will be recalled, they contended that it is unnecessary and therefore undesirable to treat the problems of discrimination and prejudice at school when students are unaware of them. The problem thus remains unresolved since children eventually will become not only aware of discrimination against Burakumin but will also be indoctrinated with prejudice toward the minority members by a number of socialization agents. Thus latent prejudice in childhood leads sooner or later to overt forms of prejudice if nothing is done to curb it.

How shall Junanese proceed from here? What direction should they seek? Instrumental to the introduction of Burakumin's responses to this question may be one of the items in the value survey (Brameld 1968: 278–298) administered by our research team to the Junanese (102 households), randomly selected respondents (100 households) in Eizen at large, the prefectural leader respondents (16 persons), and two other groups. The item reads as follows:

Taro-san [Mr. Taro] just graduated from junior high school. He lives in a rural community of Burakumin (minority people). His uncle, a shoemaker, urges Taro-san to work for him.
  a. Taro-san should seek a job in Osaka but tell no one where he is from.
  b. He should stay in his community where he feels secure among friends and relatives.
  c. He should seek a job in Osaka but struggle proudly with other Burakumin for full emancipation.

Each respondent was asked to check whichever one of the three choices comes nearest to expressing his own belief. Eighty-seven per cent of the Junanese respondents checked C while seven per cent chose A and only four per cent preferred B. Thus the dominant pattern of Junanese orientations indicated here supports the belief expressed in C. Yet, in this militant community of Junan, 11 per cent preferred passive invisibility. In this connection it is worthwhile to note that C was chosen by 66 per cent of Eizen (non-Burakumin) respondents at large and by 61.5 per cent of the leader respondents (only two are Burakumin). Meanwhile, twenty-seven per cent of the Eizen respondents preferred B whereby none of the leader respondents showed their preference for this alternative. Finally B was chosen by seven per cent of the former and by 30.8 per cent of the latter. It may deserve special attention to point out that one-third of the Eizen and leader respondents believed that the best choice for the Burakumin to make, given the above situation, is either A or B. Yet, it is significant that the majority chose C even though this choice is not necessarily consistent with their practice.

What ought to be done to realize Junanese's belief that the Burakumin should struggle proudly with other Burakumin for full emancipation? Their responses are epitomized here.

(1) Self-reliance was stressed time and again by Burakumin Socialist Hikino, a successful slipper maker, with whom we were acquainted in previous chapters. Hikino pointed out that the Junanese who tend to

be parasitic and irresponsible must learn to become economically self-reliant in order to achieve real emancipation. Another Junanese further argued that growth of self-strength (Jiriki) is one necessary condition for emancipation. There are several Burakumin communities in Kagada -ken which are not dependent upon welfare aid and the governmental employment program. According to Hikino, one of them is a farming village near Eizen where people are unusually frugal and industrious. Another community with which we are acquainted is a much smaller group of Burakumin than Junan which succeeded in becoming self-reliant, located several miles from Takatsu, the capital of Kagada. In this community a glove factory provides jobs for more than 30 Burakumin families. Kaihōdōmei Leader Yoshino who invited us to the community said that only two families in the entire community are dependent on welfare aid.

(2) Complementary to growth of self-reliance in the struggles for emancipation, Hikino and Kaihōdōmei members agreed, is what was termed Gyōsei Tōsō the struggle for emancipation through political channels. The strategy here is to put pressure upon administration and political groups to meet Burakumin demands. Through this struggle, the Junanese "acquired" welfare, unemployment, medical, and educational aid; a playground, a bathhouse, a running water system, and a half dozen apartments built in Junan. The Junanese are pressing further for the "abolition" of Burakumin unemployment and the improvement of living standards. In Dōwakai Leader Notsu's view, the improvement of economic conditions is an essential path to the assimilation of Burakumin into the larger society and, in this respect, persuasive political action is vital. Incidentally, Dōwakai seeks political persuasion to implement Burakumin policies whereas Kaihōdōmei presupposes political polarization in which Tōsō (struggle) is encouraged. Accordingly Gyōsei Tōsō is a Kaihōdōmei tactic. Both Kaihōdōmei and Dōwakai, which disagree on vital issues and policy, agree on the immediate objectives of Gyōsei Tōsō and political persuasion though political channels are often different. Hikino warned that Gyōsei Tōsō, nevertheless, should be a means toward self-reliance.

Discrimination against minority members is unconstitutional under the Constitution of Japan adopted in 1947. For example, Article 14 states: "All of the people are equal under the law, and there shall be no recrimination in political, economic or social relations because of race, creed, sex, social status or family origin." Yet Gyōsei Tōsō has not attempted to test the unconstitutionality of discrimination in the

Supreme Court; nor has it tried to attack discriminatory practices in employment by introducing anti-discriminatory laws. In the opinion of a few prefectural leader informants of our research team including Kaihōdōmei Leader Yoshino and Dōwakai Leader Notsu, illegalization of discriminatory practices would be impractical because anti-discriminatory laws, even if imposed upon employers, would not be effectively enforced. It is the contention of Yoshino that a more effective approach would be to educate employers and the public in general to correct their evil practice of discrimination while continuing with Gyōsei Tōsō to force political agents to implement Burakumin demands.

Extralegally, Kaihōdōmei at the national as well as at the local levels seeks cooperation for anti-discrimination from labor unions and placement offices. A left-wing labor union leader informant told us that such cooperation is practiced between Kaihōdōmei and his union. Although we could not detect it in Kagada-ken, Kaihōdōmei and public placement offices in Kyoto cooperate to prevent discrimination in employment.

(3) It should be pointed out that community unity, as many Burakumin agreed, is most vital to their concerted efforts for emancipation through either political persuasion or Gyōsei Tōsō. It may also be conducive to the encouragement of self-reliance. Intra-group conflicts reduced in many ways the effectiveness not only of Junanese struggles for community improvement but also of their strategies for influencing city hall and other social-political agents. It will be remembered that the integration of Junanese into Japanese life is one of their cherished hopes.

(4) The development of Burakumin Gakuryoku (academic ability) is the fourth response to our question at the outset. In the Zendōkyō conference we attended the cultivation of Gakuryoku of Burakumin children was frequently stressed. Junanese are also aware of the vital import of Gakuryoku as an antecedent to getting better jobs. To be sure, Kaihōdōmei Leader Yoshino and Burakumin P.T.A. Member Okano did not fail to mention Gakuryoku. Particularly does Burakumin Gakuryoku become a serious concern when compulsory education is polarized as in Tōzai Junior High School as well as in many other junior high schools, due to the excessive emphasis upon preparatory education which alienates Junanese students from the majority of students. If Burakumin Hikino's notion of self-reliance is to be fully realized, Junan must certainly compete with other communities by graduating Junanese boys and girls from senior high schools with the rate comparable to that (85%) of non-Burakumin communities.

Adequate formal education and the improvement of Gakuryoku are a concern of Burakumin national organizations, both Kaihōdōmei and Dōwakai. Above all, Kaihōdōmei is extremely critical of present educational practice since, in its view, present compulsory education fails to provide democratic learning and teaching. In compulsory education, we have seen, Burakumin have suffered discrimination and alienation. In Tōzai Junior High School, effective attempts have seldom been accomplished to reduce competitive practice and pressures for preparatory education from which they gain little. This is not to say, however, that schools have entirely failed to respond to Burakumin needs. At Yonami Elementary School, it will be remembered, continuously constructive efforts were made to develop Burakumin Gakuryoku as part of Dōwa education.

Some years ago Yonami Elementary School teachers were involved in Burakumin children's club activities during which the abacus and various forms of recreation were taught. Prior to becoming a Kaihōdōmei executive, Yoshino himself volunteered to tutor Junanese children in the Junan Community Center. Unfortunately these efforts were often disrupted and therefore did not last for a long time.

Burakumin organizations, particularly Kaihōdōmei, played an important role in pressing the prefectural government to provide scholarships to Burakumin in order to encourage them to go to senior high schools. Kagada Prefectural Government and municipal governments together provide 140 scholarships covering 50 per cent of Burakumin high school students. The amount of each scholarship per month is $ 4.00. Additionally, 290 scholarships (each being $ 8.00) are granted only once a year to the first and seventh grade Burakumin students entering elementary schools and junior high schools respectively. These scholarships cover 60 per cent of Burakumin first and seventh graders in Kagada-ken. Junanese students receive these two types of scholarships along with Burakumin students in other communities. These scholarships, however, are too small to substantially improve Burakumin education unless the stipends are increased in the future.

In terms of informal education, a job-training program is presently under way with prefectural and municipal funds. Over $ 8,000 was appropriated in a single year for job-training on which the focus was a driver training program through which about 150 young Burakumin could be qualified as drivers. Again Burakumin pressures were largely responsible for the launching of this program.

(5) Finally, intermarriage is viewed by Burakumin as desirable al-

though it is abhorred by the majority of non-Burakumin. The ultimate resolution of discrimination, said one Junanese, will consist in free intermarriage between Burakumin and non-Burakumin until distinctions between them completely disappear. Studies and books on Burakumin which we became acquainted with did not describe any single case of intermarriage causing Burakumin opposition on the ground that spouses were non-Burakumin. Opposition to marriage with non-Burakumin was not posed by any Junanese, as far as we could detect in Junan where over 50 men married non-Burakumin women including wives of our Kaihōdōmei leader, Socialist Hikino, and P.T.A. informant Okano. Some of these wives told us they were warmly accepted and respected by the community. Hence refusal of intermarriage by non-Burakumin is considered one of the most indigenous, tenacious causes of discrimination. Prejudice toward free intermarriage is perceived by Burakumin as the most difficult impediment to full emancipation. There is no omnipotent antidote to the deep-seated prejudice against minority members. Yet education, Kaihōdōmei-affiliated Burakumin agreed, is one of the essential means toward the resolution of prejudice if education is effectively used. Their reference to education leads us to the last topic.

(6) Our question here is what kind of Dōwa education is most needed in an attempt to dissolve prejudice? Perhaps practical approaches to this question can be arbitrarily categorized as follows. The first is the approach adopted by Tōzai Junior High School. This, it will be recalled, is based upon the assumption that since students, Burakumin and non-Burakumin, do not have prejudice toward each other, it is unnecessary or even undesirable to expose young students unaware of Burakumin to the history and contemporary evil of prejudice and discrimination against minority members. It also optimistically assumes that Burakumin will be eventually forgotten if minority members themselves endeavor to correct erratic, irresponsible, and aggressive attitudes and behavior.

The second we called the indirect approach. In this approach there is a high degree of sensitivity toward the reality of prejudice toward Burakumin but teachers adopting this approach are not yet convinced that children are mature enough to understand the nature of prejudice if discriminatory problems are directly treated at school. Furthermore, they are not sure whether they can obtain Burakumin support to dissect highly sensitive problems whose mistreatment tends to cause severe criticism. Nevertheless, Yonami teachers together with other teachers believed that through the treatment of social problems and problems of human relations among children in the "special class discussion" without particular reference to Burakumin, children will be helped to become sensitive toward each other as well as to social problems.

The third is the Gakuryoku approach which emphasizes the growth of Burakumin Gakuryoku as the focus of Dōwa education. The intention of this approach, as we mentioned, is to improve intellectual ability of Burakumin students so that more Burakumin can receive senior high school education. A number of Kyoto junior high schools, for example, emphasize Gakuryoku development. The last approach attempts to introduce Burakumin history and contemporary life into curriculums in order to acquaint students with Burakumin problems in both historical and contemporary perspectives. The assumption of this approach, contrary to that of the first approach, is that understanding of minority problems will lead toward the resolution of prejudice. We recall that left-oriented Kaihōdōmei Junanese advocated this approach while Dōwakai-oriented parents did not support it.

In practice these approaches are not separable; rather, they are related to each other in the development of Dōwa education. For example, Yonami Elementary School paid attention to the indirect treatment of problems as well as to Gakuryoku development and also considered a possibility of developing the last approach. Many Kyoto schools reveal a similar situation. But Junanese themselves have not agreed as to which path should constitute the central approach to the question of prejudice. Nor have teachers achieved any consensus on this question. It may be said that whichever direction Junanese deem to be most effective, their concerted support for the development of the chosen approach will help the schools of Junanese innovate Dōwa education.

By way of comparison, let us look at Kyoto Dōwa education. We visited Kyoto several times for interviews with school board members, teachers, principals, and Zendōkyō officials in order to gain a perspective on the problem.

Zendōkyō and Kyoto-fu (Greater Kyoto including the city of Kyoto and surrounding municipalities) School Board which is equivalent to a prefectural school board, have developed remarkable cooperation in building a theoretical framework and practical programs for Dōwa education. In political orientation and understanding of Burakumin problems, they are much more advanced than any other school boards and Zendōkyō chapters elsewhere in Japan. Kyoto Municipal School Board cooperates, perhaps under the influence of Kyoto-fu School

Board, with Zendōkyō in developing Dōwa education, but politically it is less closely allied with Zendōkyō. Thus radical teachers, we were told, tend to be relegated to local posts. Nevertheless, the Kyoto Municipal School Board spokesman on Dōwa education presented a no less radical view than that of Zendōkyō.

In Kyoto the practical task of Dōwa education is understood as the development of ability to cope with social and personal problems. Our interviewees felt concertedly that one of the toughest problems of the disfranchised children is their lack of ability to fulfill intellectual exercise such as reading, writing, and counting. One of the major concerns of Dōwa education is said to be the development of Gakuryoku which is required for better jobs and promotion to senior high schools. Particularly, admission of a greater number of Burakumin to the institutions of higher education, said our interviewees, is a first step for emancipation. Hence a systematic tutoring program has been developed since 1952. For example, at Rakube Junior High School accommodating 43 Burakumin students, all faculty members are required to participate in tutoring Burakumin. Four hours per week are devoted to tutoring which takes place in Burakumin community centers. Not only are special subjects taught but problems of prejudice and discrimination as they arise are also discussed between teachers and students. The Kyoto Municipal School Board, we were told, also requires other Kyoto schools of both elementary and junior high school levels enrolling Burakumin and other disfranchised children to provide four-hour tutoring every week. According to an official of the school board, extra-preparatory tutoring for high school entrance examinations such as the one with which we are familiar at Tōzai Junior High School, was abolished at the public compulsory school level. This would make teachers active participants in Dōwa education programs.

Speaking of Burakumin ability to cope with personal problems, comments made by two elementary school principals deserve attention. Incidentally, one of the principals supervises a school whose total enrollment is predominantly Burakumin. One major task in Dōwa education at their schools is to help Burakumin form social-emotional habit patterns which, in their view, are seriously neglected at home. Training for cleanliness, language, and social manner, and the cultivation of emotional stability and self-confidence were pointed out. Extra-curricular activities, therefore, are emphasized. Self-confidence was fostered, the principal of the predominantly Burakumin school said, through annual all-Kyoto calligraphy contests and track races in which his school won first place. Gardening is encouraged for emotional training.

Another major concern in Dōwa education is sensitivity training through which to deepen understanding of each other's personal problems. Teachers are involved in an informal program called Seikatsu Shidō or "life-guidance" through which they counsel Burakumin students. One junior high school teacher developed "special class activity" for the frank and honest discussion of personal problems to promote understanding of each other by the use of students' diaries. Another elementary school teacher endeavored to create opportunities in social studies to understand real lives of Burakumin and their sociocultural environments.

Burakumin history and their contemporary life are not incorporated into curriculums of any level. Nor is there a project where a systematic treatment of prejudice and discrimination against the minority members is introduced. More than a half dozen of teachers and principals agreed that teachers are simply unable to treat objectively and systematically such sensitive problems since they are not trained enough for it. Meanwhile, others doubted the effectiveness of such an approach to Burakumin problems. They feared that treatment of prejudice by incompetent teachers might rather increase prejudice. In fact, one principal cited past examples of failure when some teachers in Kyoto tried to teach Burakumin history. Nevertheless, all our interviewees emphasized that when a discriminatory incident occurs among students, it should be treated thoroughly as an educational opportunity to correct prejudice and discrimination.

Finally, in order to correct inadequacy of teacher training with respect to Dōwa education, Kyoto Municipal School Board, according to its spokesman on Dōwa education, is planning to develop a city-wide inservice training program. This spokesman felt this would greatly contribute to the development of more effective Dōwa education in Kyoto.

Humiliation, despair, and alienation have wounded the lives of Burakumin one generation after another. Yet Burakumin's struggles for life were hardly exhausted when their freedom was shackled by feudalism, powerful social sanctions of feudal remnants, and long-seated prejudice. Their struggles continue to challenge the deepest sources of their strength, dignity, and hope for humanity. Thus at the founding of Suiheisha (Ninomiya 1933: 128) it was declared that:

Our ancestors worshipped freedom and equality, and practiced these principles; they were the victims of despicable class rule; they were manly martyrs of industry; they were skinned alive in recompense for their work in skinning animals;

their warm hearts were ripped out as the price for stabbing the hearts of animals; and they were spat at with the spittles of ridicule. Yet, all through these cursed nights of evil dreams, the glorious human blood has kept on flowing. And we, who have been born of this blood, have come to live in an age when men may turn into gods. The time has come when the oppressed shall throw off the brand-mark of martyrdom, and the martyr with the crown of thorns shall receive bless-ing.

This manifesto of 1922 remains to be a declaration of Burakumin struggles in the 60's. How many Japanese know this manifesto, a desparate appeal for full emancipation? How many non-Burakumin know the misery of the invisible race? How can education respond more effectively to Burakumin aspirations? The introduction of Dōwa education is a vital matter in Japanese culture if the inequalities and injustices long inflicted upon Burakumin are to be thoroughly eli-minated.

BIBLIOGRAPHY

Brameld, Theodore, 1968, *Japan: Culture, Education and Change In Two Communities*. New York: Holt, Rinehart, and Winston.

De Vos, George, and Hiroshi Wagatsuma, (Eds.), 1966, *Japan's Invisible Race: Caste in Culture and Personality*. Berkeley: University of California Press.

Fujitani, Toshio, 1954, "Modern History of Baraku" in *Baraku History and Emancipation Movement*. (Ed.). Kiyoshi Inoue, Kyoto: Buraku Mondai Kenkyūsho.

Inoue, Kiyoshi, 1964, *The Study of Buraku Problems: History and Theory of Emancipation*. Kyoto: Buraku Mondai Kenkyūsho.

Kadōkyō, 1964, *The Material for General Assembly in 1964*. Takatsu: Kadōkyō.

Ministry of Education (Monbushō), 1965, *The Real Situation of Dōwa Education at Schools*. Tokyo: Ministry of Education.

Morito, Tatsuo, 1961, *Prospect and Retrospect of Japanese Education*. Tokyo: Minshu Kyōiku Kyōgikai.

Ninomiya, Shigeaki, 1933, "An Inquiry Concerning the Origin, Development, and Present Situation of the Eta in Relation to the History of Social Classes in Japan," in *The Transactions of the Asiatic Society of Japan*. Second Series, Vol. X.

Ogawa, Tarō, 1964, *Study of Dōwa Education*. Kyoto: Buraku Mondai Kenkyūsho

Reischauer, Edwin, 1967, *Beyond Vietnam: The United States and Asia*. New York: Vintage Book.

Shimahara, Nobuo, 1967, *A Study of the Enculturative Roles of Japanese Education*. Unpublished Doctoral Dissertation. Boston: Boston University Library.

Singleton, John, 1967, *Nichū: A Japanese School*. New York: Holt, Rinehart and Winston.

Tōjō, Takashi, 1962, "Advancement of Dōwa Education," in *Manual of Dōwa Education*. Buraku Mondai Kenkyūsho. Kyoto: Buraku Mondai Kenkyūsho.

Zendōkyō, 1964, *Materials for National Dōwa Education Study Conference*. Kyoto: Zendōkyō.

RECOMMENDED READING

* The books with the star mark are written in Japanese.

Bearsley, Richard, John Hall, and Robert Ward, 1959, *Village Japan*. Chicago: University of Chicago Press.

Benedict, Ruth, 1946, *Chrysanthemum and the Sward*. Boston: Houghton Mifflin Co.

Brameld, Theodore, 1968, *Japan: Culture, Education and Change in Two Communities*. New York: Holt, Rinehart, and Winston, Inc.

*Buraku Kaihōdōmei, 1970, *Buraku Emancipation Movement*. Osaka: Buraku Kaihōdōmei.

*Buraku Mondai Kenkyūsho, 1962, *Manual of Dowa Education*. Kyoto: Buraku Mondai Kenkyūsho.

*——, 1970, *History of Buraku and Emancipation Movement*. Kyoto: Buraku Mondai Kenkyūsho.

Cornell, John, and Robert Smith, 1956, *Two Japanese Villages*. Ann Arbor: University of Michigan Press.

De Vos, George, and Hiroshi Wagatsuma, (Eds.), 1966, *Japan's Invisible Race: Caste in Culture and Personality*. Berkeley: University of California Press.

*Fujitani, Toshio, 1954, "Modern History of Buraku," in *Buraku History and Emancipation Movement*. (Ed.) Kiyoshi Inoue. Kyoto: Baruku Mondai Kenkyūsho.

*Fukuchi, Kōzō, and Kōzō Nakamaru, (Eds.), 1969, *Practice of Emancipation Education*. Vols. I–IV. Tokyo: Meiji Tosho.

*Fukutake, Tadashi, 1961, *Japanese Rural Society*. Tokyo: Tokyo University Press.

*——, 1961, *Japanese Society*. Tokyo: Yuhido.

*Funayama, Kenji, 1963, *History of Controversies in Postwar Japanese Education: Perspectives of Thought in Postwar Education*. Tokyo: Tōyōkan.

Hall, John, and Richard Beardsley, 1965, *Twelve Doors to Japan*. New York: MacGraw-Hill, Inc.

*Horimatsu, Takeichi, 1959, *Modern History of Japanese Education*. Tokyo: Risōsha.

*Inoue, Kiyoshi, 1964, *The Study of Buraku Problems: History and Theory of Emancipation*. Kyoto: Buraku Mondai Kenkyūsho.

*——, 1969, *History of Buraku and Theory of Emancipation*. Tokyo: Hatada Shoten.

*Kadōkyō, 1964, *The Material For General Assembly in 1964*. Takatsu, Kagada: Kadōkyō.

*Kaigo, Katsuo, 1957, *New Japanese Moral Education*. Tokyo: Seibundo Shinkōsha.

*Karasawa, Tomitarō, 1958, *Creation of New Moral Education*. Tokyo: Tōyōkan.

*Koyama, Takashi, 1960, *Study of the Contemporary Family*. Tokyo: Kōbundō.

*Ministry of Education (Monbushō), 1965, *The Real Situation of Dowa Education At Schools*. Tokyo: Monbushō.

*Miyahara, Seiichi, (Ed.), 1961, *History of Education*. Tokyo: Minshu Kyōiku Kyōgikai.

Morito, Tatsuo, 1961, *Prospect and Retrospect of Japanese Education*. Tokyo: Minshu Kyōiku Kyōgikai.

Ninomiya, Shigeaki, 1933, "An Inquiry Concerning the Origin, Development, and Present Situation of the Eta in Relation to the History of Social Classes in Japan," in *The Transactions of the Asiatic Society of Japan*. Second Series, Vol. X.

*Ogawa, Tarō, 1964, *Study of Dōwa Education*. Kyōto: Buraku Mondai Kenkyūsho.

*Ōkochi, Kazuo, 1951, *The Analysis of the Situation of Postwar Society*. Tokyo: Nippon Hyōronsha.

Passin, Herbert, 1965, *Society and Education in Japan*. New York: Bureau of Publications, Teachers College, Columbia University.

Reischauer, Edwin, 1964, *Japan: Past and Present*, 3rd ed. New York: Alfred Knopf, Inc.

——, 1967, *Beyond Vietnam: The United States and Asia*. New York: Vintage Book.

Shimahara, Nobuo, 1967, *A Study of the Enculturative Roles of Japanese Education*. Unpublished Doctoral Dissertation. Boston: Boston University Library.

Singleton, John, 1967, *Nichū: A Japanese School*. New York: Holt, Rinehart and Winston, Inc.

*Suzuki, Sōken, 1964, *Japanese Modernization and the Thought of On*. Kyoto: Hōritsu Bunkasha.

*Taniguchi, Shūtarō, and Ichirō Hirano, 1960, *Personality Image of Buraku*. Tokyo: Sanichi Shobō.

*Tōjō, Takashi, "Advancement of Dōwa Education," in *Manual of Dōwa Education*. Buraku Mondai Kenkyusho. Kyoto: Buraku Mondai Kenkyusho.

*——, 1964, *Introduction to Dowa Education*. Kyoto: Sekibunsha.

*Yamamoto, Noboru, 1966, *Sociological Study of Buraku Discrimination*. Kyoto: Buraku Mondai Kenkyūsho.

*Yanaibara, Tadao, (Ed.), 1958, *The Overview of Postwar Japanese History*. Vols. I and II. Tokyo: Tokyo University Press.

*Zendōkyō, 1964, *Materials for National Dōwa Education Study Conference*. Kyoto: Zendōkyō.

GLOSSARY OF JAPANESE TERMS

Bisaku Heiminkai	Burakumin Self-Improvement Association
Bunke	a branch house
Buraku Kaihō Zenkoku Iinkai	Burakumin Emancipation National Committee
Burakumin	a Japanese minority
Buraku Kaihōdōmei	Burakumin Emancipation League
Buraku Mondai Kenkyūsho	Institute for the Study of Burakumin Problems
Buraku Mondai ni Furenai	not to touch Burakumin problems
Buraku no Hito	Burakumin
Bushi	warriors
Chasen	a pariah group
Chūse	a period between 1192–1603
Do-Hi	Do: male slaves, Hi: female slaves
Dōwa education	education for emancipation
Dōwakai	a shortened term for Nippon Dōwakai
Dōwa Kyōiku	Dōwa education
Eizen	a fictitious name of a city
Eta Seibatsu	Eta extermination
Etori	a collector of meat for hawks and dogs
Fuzoku	being attached
Furenai	do not touch
Gakkō Gyōji	general school programs
Gakkyūkai	special class activities, free discussion periods for elementary school pupils
Gakkyū Katsudō	special class activities for junior high school students
Gakuryoku	academic ability
Ganbari	endurance
Genin	temple and private slaves
Giri	mutual obligation
Gyōsei Tōsō	administration struggle, struggle against policies of municipal and prefectural governments
Hachiya	a pariah group
Hinin	a non-human being
Hirohito	Emperor since 1926
Hokkaidō	a major northern island of Japan
Honke	a main house
Honshū	a Japanese main island
Imakawa	a Samurai ruler

Jichikai	a self-governing association
Jirō	All Japan Free Labor Union
Jūdō	a Japanese sport
Junan	a fictitious name of a Burakumin community
Junanese	Junan Burakumin
Kadōkyō	a shortened term for Kagada Dōwa Kyōiku Kenkyū Kyōgikai
Kagada	a fictitious name of a prefecture
Kagada Dōwa Kyōiku Kenkyū Kyōgikai	Kagada Dōwa Education Study Association
Kaihōdōmei	a shortened term for Buraku Kaihōdōmei
Kaihō Iinkai	a shortened term for Buraku Kaihō Zenkoku Iinkai
Kankō	government cultivators
Karate	a Japanese sport
Kawara Mono	a pariah group
Keimō Katsudō	enlightening activities
Kendō	a Japanese sport
Komai, Kisaku	a Burakumin leader
Kōchi	a prefecture
Kodomokai	children's clubs
Kokutai Shugi	nationalism for the development of the Emperor state
Kotani	a fictitious name of a community
Kūhō	a fictitious name of a priest
Kumi	smaller units of Jichikai
Kunuhi	government servants
Kyoto-fu	Greater Kyoto
Kyūshū	a major southern island of Japan
Matsumoto, Jiichirō	a Burakumin leader
Meiji	a period between 1868–1912
Miyoshi, Iheiji	a Burakumin leader
Monzenmachi	a town of temples
Motoda	a Meiji Confucian
Mukōjima	an island on the opposite side
Mutsuhito	Meiji Emperor during 1868–1912
Nagasaki	a prefecture
Nakae, Chōmin	a supporter of Burakumin emancipation
Netako o Okosuna	do not wake up the sleeping child
Nichiren	a sect of Buddhism
Ninja Gumi	a Burakumin children's club
Nippon Dōwakai	Japanese Burakumin Assimilation Association
Okayama	a prefecture
On	obligation, kindness, favor
Onbo	a pariah group
Osoroshii	fearful
Rakube	a fictitious name of a Kyoto junior high school
Renga	bricks
Ritsuryō (system)	a political system dominant in the 7th and 8th century
Ryōmin	good people
Ryōtō	tomb guards
Saikō, Mankichi	a Burakumin leader

Sakamoto, Seiichirō	a Burakumin leader
Sanjo	a pariah group
Sano, Mankichi	a supporter of Burakumin emancipation
Samurai	warriors
Sarariiman	a white collar worker
Sasayaki	a Yonamai Elementry School document
Seikatsu Shidō	guidance
Seikatsu to Kenkō o Mamoru Kai	Association for the Protection of Health and Living
Seitokai	a student self-governing association
Senmin	lowly people
Shi	four
Shikoku	the fourth largest island of Japan
Shimazaki	a novelist
Shin Heimin	new commoners
Shinju	a fictitious name of a city
Shinuhi	private slaves
Shiromachi	a fictitious name of the city
Shittai	a governmental program for the unemployed
Shōwa	a period starting from 1926
Shūban	a student patrol
Shūgaku Ryokō	a trip for learning
Shūshin	moral education
Sōkagakkai	a religious group
Suiheisha	Levellers' Movement
Taika Restoration	a political reform in 701
Taishō	a period between 1912–1926
Takarazuka	a theatre
Takatsu	a fictitious name of a city
Takatsukasa	Department of Falconry
Takusan no Mondai o Okosu	create many problems
Tatami	straw mats
Tennō	Emperor
Tesshin Dōshikai	Iron-mind Comrade Association
Tokkatsu	a shortened form of Tokubetsu Kyōiku Katsudō
Tokubetsu Kyōiku Katsudō	special education activities
Tokugawa	a period between 1603–1867
Tokushima	a prefecture
Tokushu Buraku	a special Burakumin community
Tokushu Burakumin	special village people
Tonai	a pariah group
Tōsō	struggle
Tōzai	a fictitious name of a junior high school
Tsubo	1.8 square meters
Ube	a fictitious name for a fishing village
Ueda, Otoichi	a Burakumin leader
Yonami	a fictitious name of a community
Yottsu	four
Yūwa	conciliation
Yūwa Education	education for assimilation
Zakko	a pariah group

Zendōkyō	a shortened term for Zenkoku Dōwa Kyōiku Kenkyū Kyōgikai
Zenjin Kyōiku	whole-man education
Zenkoku Dōwa Kyōiku Kenkyū Kyōgikai	National Dōwa Education Study Association